HEIRLOOM
MACHINE SEWING
for QUILTERS

Susan Stewart

American Quilter's Society
P. O. Box 3290 • Paducah, KY 42002-3290
FAX: 270-898-1173 *www.AmericanQuilter.com*

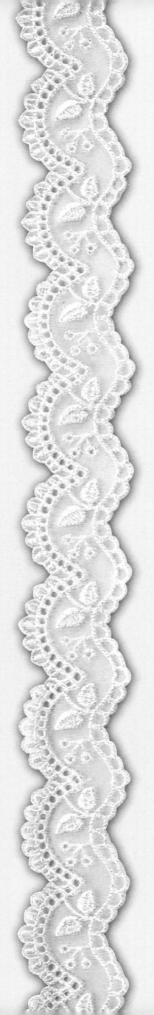

Located in Paducah, Kentucky, the American Quilter's Society (AQS) is dedicated to promoting the accomplishments of today's quilters. Through its publications and events, AQS strives to honor today's quiltmakers and their work and to inspire future creativity and innovation in quiltmaking.

Editor: Barbara Smith
Graphic Design: Mary Beth Head
Cover Design: Michael Buckingham
Photography: Charles R. Lynch

Library of Congress Cataloging-in-Publication Data

Stewart, Susan, 1955-
      Heirloom machine sewing for quilters / by Susan Stewart.
          p. cm.
      Summary: "Learn to incorporate traditional heirloom fabrics and sewing techniques into a variety of quilts and quilted projects. Projects for home decor, gift giving, and personal use. Detailed instructions, templates, illustrations and how-to photographs provided"--Provided by publisher.
      ISBN 978-1-57432-944-5
      1. Patchwork--Patterns. 2. Machine quilting--Patterns. I. Title.

      TT835.S73135 2007
      746.46'041--dc22

                        2007040742

      Additional copies of this book may be ordered from the American Quilter's Society, PO Box 3290, Paducah, KY 42002-3290, or online at: www.AmericanQuilter.com. For phone orders only 800-626-5420. For all other inquiries, call 270-898-7903.

Proudly printed and bound in the United States of America.

Dedication

To my parents, Marvin and Gloria Meyer, who gave me a secure childhood and helped me grow up confident that I could do anything I set my sights on. Mom, you basically relinquished the sewing machine to me when I was still very young, and now, the two of you drive your motor home to meet me at quilt shows.

To my children, Annie and David, I am so very proud of both of you! May your lives be abundantly filled with love, joy, wonder, and adventure.

And most of all, to my husband, Mark, life with you is more wonderful than I ever dared to dream. You're the best! I love you dearly.

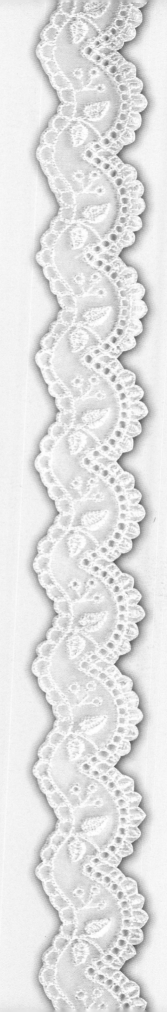

Acknowledgments

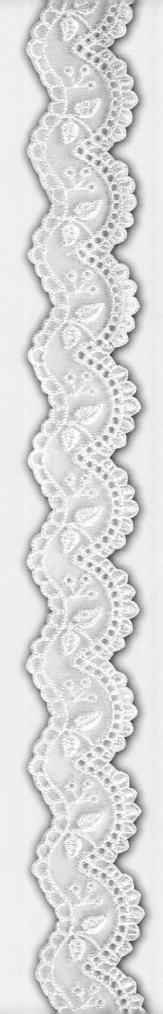

I am grateful to these businesses and individuals for their support:

Pfaff, Bernina, Husqvarna Viking, and Baby Lock sewing machine companies, for providing their wonderful sewing machines for me to use all these years;

YLI Corporation, for providing threads;

Zundt Design, Ltd., for providing beautifully digitized machine-embroidery designs;

Martha Pullen, for introducing me to heirloom sewing and providing me with opportunities I could never have imagined;

Linda Hayden of Hands and Heart Quilting, for longarm quilting the SPRINGTIME HEIRLOOM quilt.

Contents

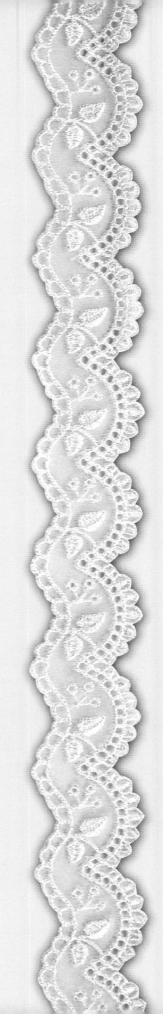

Introduction

Fabric and stitching have always fascinated me. When not quite five years old, I made a little yellow embroidered bib for my baby sister. By nine or ten, I was making many of my own clothes. I tried other needle arts, including knitting, needlepoint, and hand embroidery, but always came back to the sewing machine. I made garments for myself, my sister, my cousin, and later, my children.

Then in 1988, I had one of those moments when something happens and things are changed. I picked up a copy of an heirloom sewing magazine. I had never seen laces and fabrics like that. I was hooked. I already knew how to sew, and because I consider myself more of an engineer than an artist, it was easy to teach myself how to make those beautifully embellished children's clothes by machine. Without being taught the *proper* way of doing the techniques, I developed my own ways. Soon I was going beyond the traditional techniques and coming up with new interpretations. By 1990, I was sewing, writing, and teaching my heirloom sewing techniques professionally.

During those years, I admired quilting, but didn't do much of it. Then, I made a Christmas quilt for my husband, a fiftieth anniversary quilt for my parents, and a twenty-first birthday quilt for my daughter. The siren call of quilting was capturing me. About four years ago, as I was giving a trunk show presentation of my garments for our local quilt guild, I had another of those moments. It struck me that I was uniquely qualified to integrate heirloom sewing techniques with the exciting creativity in the quilt world. I started quilting with a passion. I have been blessed to have my quilts accepted into major shows and to win prizes.

This book contains many of the heirloom sewing by machine techniques that I learned, developed, and modified over the past eighteen years. They make beautiful, unique quilts, with looks that can be soft and romantic, like the lace used in them, or brighter and more modern. The techniques you learn here can also be used for garments and non-quilted items. Try these techniques and explore what you can do with them. But beware … heirloom sewing can be habit-forming!

Heirloom Sewing Techniques

∼ FABRICS, LACES, AND NOTIONS ∽

The heirloom sewing techniques used in these quilts were adapted from techniques used primarily for children's clothing. Cotton batiste and cotton laces are the standards for heirloom sewing, and these translate well into quilting. Let's look at suitable fabrics and supplies:

Batiste ❧ This is a lightweight, plain weave, soft, semi-sheer fabric. Most of the quilts and other projects have sections of embellished batiste that have been layered over quilting cotton. The fabric underneath shows through the batiste, creating several color values.

One hundred percent cotton batiste is preferable to poly-cotton blends, because the blends tend to pucker and fray. Swiss cotton batiste is the gold standard for heirloom sewing for pieces such as christening gowns, but it is quite expensive. For quilts, less expensive domestic 100 percent cotton batiste works just as well. It is usually available in white, ivory, and pastels.

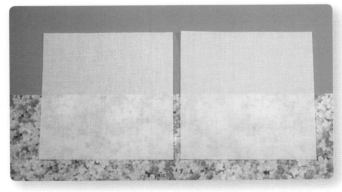

Left, *Swiss cotton batiste;* right, *domestic cotton batiste*

Organdy and organza ❧ These are sheer, lightweight, crisp fabrics. The finest organdy is Swiss cotton. It is crisper than organza, which is usually made of silk or synthetics. The natural-fiber fabrics are recommended. They are available in white, ivory, and occasionally pastels and dark colors.

Left, *Swiss cotton organdy;* right, *silk organza*

Handkerchief linen ❧ A lightweight, even-weave linen fabric, it is available in many qualities and in linen-cotton blends. This fabric is used for appliqués and appliquéd bias strips, but in all the projects, quilting cotton may be substituted for the linen.

Netting ❧ These open-weave, transparent fabrics have tiny diamond or octagonal holes throughout. One hundred percent cotton English netting was used for the samples in the photos. It has larger holes than silk or nylon netting or tulle. It is very soft, and when combined with decorative machine stitching, it makes beautiful machine-made lace. It is expensive, but a little goes a long way. Allow for approximately 25 percent shrinkage.

Silk bridal illusion is very soft and fine but even more expensive than cotton netting. Nylon tulle is inexpensive and will work for the techniques given here, although it is somewhat scratchy. Beware of hot irons when using this fabric!

English netting is available in white, ivory, and occasionally black. Nylon tulle is available in every color of the rainbow.

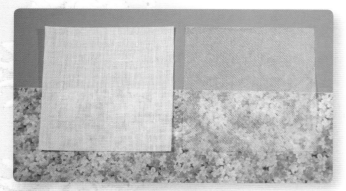

Left, *handkerchief linen;* right, *English cotton netting*

Underlayer fabric ❧ A lot of 100 percent cotton quilt fabrics are suitable for the layer of fabric under the embellished batiste. When shopping for this fabric, take your batiste with you to see how it looks when layered. Colors can be surprising. Some shadow through beautifully, while others look muddy, and I haven't yet found a sure-fire way to predict what looks best. I think ivory batiste often looks better with fabrics other than bright white, unless it is tea-dyed to tone down the brightness. Choose subtle marbled and tonal fabrics, because busy prints can overwhelm the embellishments on the batiste.

Lace ❧ Traditional heirloom sewers use French Valenciennes and English laces. Antique laces are 100 percent cotton, while newer laces have five to ten percent nylon added for strength. These laces are beautiful, very soft, and not scratchy. They are stronger and more durable than they appear. Lace that has two straight sides is meant to have fabric stitched on both sides and is called "insertion lace."

Insertion laces

Edging lace has one straight side and one scalloped side. The straight side is stitched to a fabric.

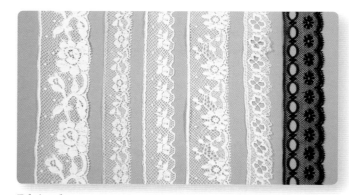

Edging laces

Along the straight edges of the lace are three or four heavier threads. This heavier area is called the "header" or "heading." Most laces can be gathered by pulling one or more of the header threads. For shaped lace techniques, having a header thread that can be pulled is a requirement. Laces other than French or English cotton could be used for many of the techniques given here, but stick with good quality lace, not nylon seam binding lace on a card. Cotton laces are available in white, ivory, and occasionally black.

Thread ❧ The threads for these lightweight materials must also be lightweight, so that the stitching does not detract from the lace and other embellishments. It should be 100 percent cotton, as fine as you can find, in a color to match the lace or batiste. Use the same thread in both the needle and bobbin.

Some recommended threads
- YLI Heirloom cotton #100/2
- YLI Heirloom cotton #70/2
- Madeira Cotona #80

A little heavier thread, but also suitable
- Mettler® #60/2
- YLI Soft Touch #60/2
- Superior MasterPiece™ #50/2
- DMC® #50

Sewing machine ❧ All of the techniques presented can be done with just a straight stitch, a zigzag, and a few decorative stitches, such as a featherstitch and tiny satin-stitch oval. Additional stitches, especially a pin stitch or Point de Paris stitch, are nice extras. An open-toed or clear foot is a good aid for visibility, and a five- or seven-groove pintuck foot is helpful for stitching twin-needle pintucks.

Sewing-machine needles ❧ Use a machine needle to match the weight of your thread. For the finest threads, use a size 60 or 65. For the slightly heavier threads, use a 70. I prefer a universal rather than a sharp, but either can be used. For a pin stitch, use a 100 universal or topstitch needle. Some sewers recommend using a wing needle, but I seldom use those because the wing needle can cut either the fabric or the lace.

Scissors ❧ Heirloom sewing requires a lot of trimming close to stitching lines. Small, sharp scissors with rounded, rather than pointed, tips make this work easier. Using small scissors can cause hand and wrist pain, so take frequent breaks.

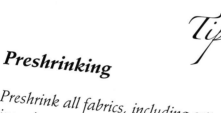

Tips

Preshrinking

Preshrink all fabrics, including cotton-embroidered insertions. Do not preshrink laces. If laces are wrinkled, steam press them without stretching them.

Starching fabrics

The fabrics used in heirloom sewing are usually very soft. Starch makes them so much easier to handle. I use one or more applications of spray starch or sizing before cutting them, and I often lightly starch them again every time I press.

∿ JOINING LACE TO LACE ↶

Use this technique to join the straight header edges of insertion and edging laces to create wider strips of lace.

Note that a dark thread was used in the samples so you can see it, but you will want to use matching thread in your pieces.

Use fine cotton thread in both the needle and bobbin and a small (size 65 or 70) needle. Place the two laces side by side, right side up if you can tell a right side, with the straight headers butted together.

With the length (L) set at 1.0 and the width (W) set at 2.5, zigzag stitch the laces together so that one swing of the needle goes over the heading of one of the laces, and the other swing of the needle goes over the heading of the other lace.

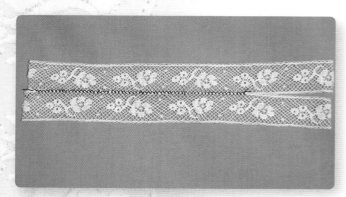

Zigzag stitch the two lace strips together.

Begin stitching about ¼" in from the cut edge of the lace to prevent the machine from "eating" the lace. Or, if necessary, start stitching with a small piece of tearaway stabilizer under the end of the lace.

If you find that your lace strips curve after stitching, it means that one strip is feeding through the machine more quickly than the other. To avoid this, use a water-soluble pen to mark regular intervals, say every 6", on both pieces of lace, then make sure that these marks match as you sew the laces together.

∿ JOINING LACE TO FABRIC ↶

Roll-and-whip method ✛ This method is suitable for stitching straight strips of lace to straight-grain edges on lightweight fabric.

Place the lightly starched fabric right side up. Place the lace strip right side down on top of the fabric, with the edge of the lace ⅛" in from the raw edge of the fabric. Zigzag (L = 1.0, W = 4.5) so that one swing of the needle stitches over the heading of the lace, and the other swing of the needle goes just off the edge of the fabric. After a few stitches, the raw fabric edge should start rolling in toward and covering the lace heading. If it doesn't, try increasing the needle thread tension slightly. Press the little rolled hem toward the fabric.

Notice how the fabric rolls toward the lace.

This next step is optional, but it gives a much neater look and keeps the little rolled seam from folding back under the lace. From the right side, zigzag (L = 1.0, W = 1.0) with a very tiny stitch so that one swing of the needle stitches over the folded edge of the fabric and into the lace, and the other swing of the needle just catches the fabric.

If you like, you can zigzag stitch the folded edge in place.

Three-step method ❧ This method can be used with bias edges and heavier fabrics.

Position the lace on top of the fabric, both right side up. Straight stitch through, and close to, both outer edges of the lace.

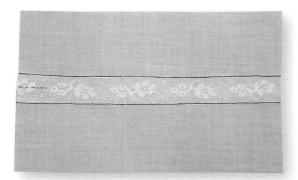

Sew the lace on top of the fabric.

On the wrong side, between the stitching lines, slit the fabric behind the lace. Press the fabric away from the lace. On the right side, zigzag stitch (L = 1.0, W = 1.5) over the lace header so that one swing of the needle goes just off the lace and into the fabric and the other swing goes into the lace. The fabric fold is caught in the stitching. Trim away the excess fabric on the wrong side close to the stitching.

Trim off the excess fabric.

∼ LACE SHAPING ∽

Many people shape lace on a cardboard or lace-shaping board by pinning the lace into the board, shaping the lace, then re-pinning the lace onto the fabric. I prefer the following method instead.

Curves

1. Trace the lace-shaping design onto starched and pressed fabric with a blue washout pen.

2. Place the fabric piece right side up on a flat surface. (You can't do this in your lap.) Pull up one of the header threads and pull some gathers in the lace so that the header thread extends several inches. Spread the gathers so the lace is not tightly bunched.

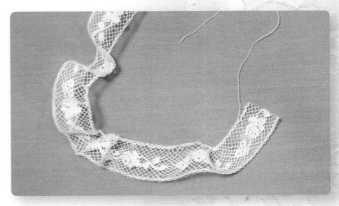

Pull a header thread to gather the lace.

3. Leaving a ½" tail, start pinning the lace to the tracing at a seam line or where the tail will be covered by another lace strip. For a smooth shape, like a circle, start pinning the lace at the bottom of the circle. Shape the lace by placing the header edge along the marked line.

4. Then, inch by inch, adjust the ease in the lace so it lies smoothly along the traced line. Pin every inch or so. Place the pins perpendicular to the lace to make them easy to remove as you stitch. The lace should have enough ease so it doesn't cup along the outer edge but not so much ease that it ruffles. Little bumps in the lace will press out later.

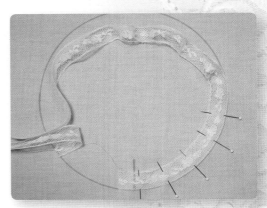

Ease the lace along the shape and pin in place.

13

5. If you have used up all the gathers and more are needed, just move several inches farther down the lace and use a pin to pull up the header thread into a loop. Pull this loop to form more gathers as needed.

6. If the shape is enclosed with no angles, like a circle, the lace must end with a seam. When the starting point at the bottom of the shape is reached, cut off the lace so it extends 1" beyond the starting point. Turn the upper end of lace under ½" and pin.

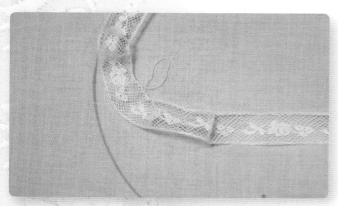

Pull up a loop of header thread to make more gathers.

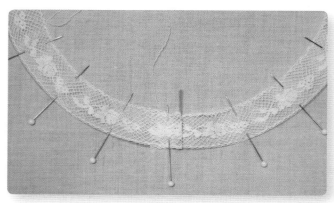

Fold the top end under ½".

Tips

Removing blue marks. I use blue water-soluble markers for everything. Soak the base fabric in plain, clear, lukewarm water. Simply spritzing the marks is not usually enough to make them disappear. Never add detergents, soap, bleach, or stain removers to the initial soak. These chemicals can set the marks. If the fabric needs to be washed to remove soil, soak it in clear water first to remove the blue marks, then launder.

Pulling up a header thread. Any of the header threads can be pulled to gather the lace, but the outer scalloped thread works best as it gives a nice, smooth edge to stitch along. Inner threads might form a tiny ruffled edge that is more difficult to stitch. Grabbing a thread is easy if you use a pin to pick up the thread about ¼" in from the cut end. Then pull the thread end out of the header so there is something to hold onto.

Angles

1. For any angles in the design, the lace strips must be mitered. Pin the lace along the traced shape, stopping 1" to 2" from the angle. Then smooth out the gathers in the unpinned lace for several inches beyond the angle.

2. At the point where the inner header crosses the angle line, fold the strip back *on top of itself*. The fold will *not* be along the angle line. Place a pin in the angle line through both layers of lace and the base fabric as shown.

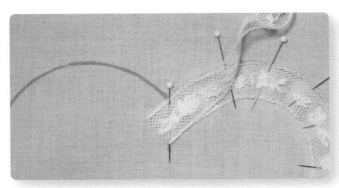

Fold the lace back on itself and pin in place on the angle.

3. Fold the lace right side up along the next leg of the angle, snug against the pin … a perfect miter and already pinned in place!

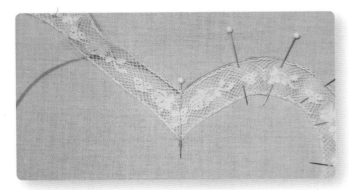

Fold the lace against the pin to complete the miter.

If the angle is less than ninety degrees, there will be a little flap of lace that extends beyond the drawn line after the miter is folded. Don't fold the flap under or cut it off at this time.

If the shape is enclosed and the lace shaping was started at an angle, a reverse miter is needed to end the lace strips. At the inner edge of the top strip, where it crosses the miter line, hold down just the header with a fingernail or pin. Fold the

top lace *under* and align its tail with the bottom strip's tail. The fold should fall right on the miter line. Pin the miter in place and trim off the top and bottom strip ends, leaving ½" tails for now.

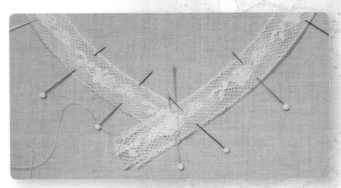

Fold the top strip along the miter line.

Stitching

1. Use very fine cotton thread (60, 80, or 100 weight) and a size 65 or 70 machine needle. Zigzag (L = 0.5–0.7, W = 2.5) over the outer header of the lace, stitching so that one swing of the needle goes just off the lace into the fabric only, and the other swing of the needle stitches over the header. Then sew the inner header in the same way.

At any angles where lace strips were begun and ended, stitch right over the lace tails. At those sharp angles where the little flap of lace is sticking out, stitch right over them. If extra gathers were pulled up, and there is a little loop of header thread, simply stitch right over that, also.

Special Heirloom Touch

Use a pin stitch (L = 2.0–2.5, W = 2.0–2.5) to attach the lace instead of a zigzag. This is a triple or quintuple straight stitch with side-to-side stitches in between. It looks like a railroad track with one side missing. Check in your manual or with a dealer to see if this stitch is on your machine. Use fine thread and a 100 or 110 universal or topstitch needle. Stitch so that the forward-and-backward portion of the stitch is in the fabric only, and the side-to-side portion of the stitch "bites" into the lace. The combination of fine thread, large needle, and repetitive stitches creates a line of tiny holes just outside the edge of the lace, similar to the traditional handwork Point de Paris stitch.

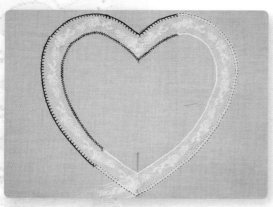

The outer lace edge is pin stitched, and the inner edge is zigzagged.

2. After stitching, trim off the lace tails and flaps, and any header thread loops, right next to the zigzag stitching.

3. Turn the fabric over. With a small, sharp (preferably blunt) scissors, trim away the fabric from behind the lace, very close to the zigzag or pin stitching.

Cut away the fabric behind the lace.

Stitch the miters and the ends.

4. From the right side, zigzag stitch over the lace miters or folded ends.

5. On the wrong side, trim away the little lace flaps behind the miters, cutting about ⅛" from the stitching.

Trimming Behind Lace

Many of the techniques in heirloom sewing require trimming fabric from behind lace. There are several things you can do to help avoid accidentally cutting the lace. First of all, use very sharp scissors that have rounded tips.

Press the fabric and lace from the wrong side just before you trim. This step seems to help by eliminating wrinkles in the fabric and the little bumps in shaped lace that can get nicked by the scissors.

I gently hold the lace and fabric together with my left hand (I'm right-handed) and slide the blade of the scissors between the lace and the fabric. With my fingers underneath the lace, I can feel the blade and can tell if it starts to go through the lace. This is hard on the wrist, so trim for only short periods of time and take frequent breaks.

When only one side of the lace is stitched down, as for an edging or a lace shape that will have an insert of embellished fabric, do not fold the lace away from the fabric to trim behind it. This stretches and distorts any lace shaping you have done. I use the same technique as before, holding the lace and fabric together with my left hand and sliding the blade of the scissors between the fabric and the lace.

Slide the scissor blade between the fabric and the lace.

~ REPAIRING LACE ~

No matter how careful you are, chances are you will occasionally cut the lace while trimming. Don't panic! It can be repaired almost invisibly.

1. Begin stitching about ½" away from the cut. Anchor the threads by zigzagging (L = 0.6–1.0, W = 2.0–2.5) over the stitched header of the lace and into the fabric.

2. When the cut is reached, stitch slowly, one stitch at a time. Stitch one swing of the needle over the header of the lace and the other swing of the needle beyond the cut into the intact part of the lace. Use your hands like a hoop on the fabric to prevent it from drawing up too much.

3. Continue one stitch at a time until the cut is closed. If the zigzag is not wide enough, make the stitch wider or reposition the presser foot a little with each stitch.

4. To finish, secure the stitching in the header of the lace for several stitches. In the figure, contrasting thread was used so you can see the repair. Use thread matching the lace for your stitches.

Repairing a tear in the lace

If you have cut a chunk out of the lace, simply place a scrap of lace under the hole, matching the lace pattern. Zigzag around the hole, and trim away the patch close to the stitching.

Repairing a hole in the lace

~ SHADOW APPLIQUÉ ~

Semi-sheer batiste allows the color of a fabric underneath it to shadow through. The bottom fabric can be the same color or a different color.

1. Trace the design onto batiste with a blue washout marker.

2. Place the shadow (appliqué) fabric under the batiste so that it extends at least ½" beyond the marked design.

3. With fine thread to match the appliqué fabric, sew on the traced line through both layers with a tiny blind-hem stitch (L = 0.5, W = 1.5). The straight part of the stitch goes on the marked line, and the side-to-side part goes toward the center of the appliqué. You could use a small zigzag (L = 1.0, W = 1.5) stitch, if you prefer.

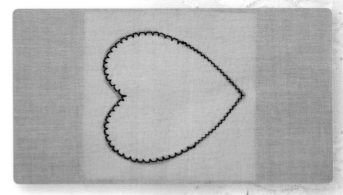

Batiste over appliqué fabric, with blind-hem stitch and zigzag

4. On the wrong side, trim away the excess fabric close to the stitching.

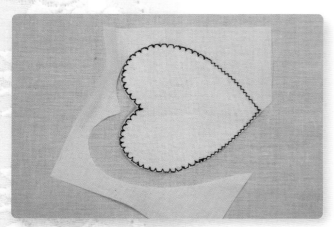

Trimming from the wrong side

∼ TWIN-NEEDLE PINTUCKS ↙

Pintuck Basics

Pintucks can be sewn to make blocks of allover textured fabric. The fabric can then be cut into strips and pieced or used as inserts inside lace shapes. Straight and shaped pintucks can be used to outline lace or appliquéd shapes or as an embellishment on their own.

1. The fabric must be soft and lightweight. Cotton batiste is ideal. Press the fabric, if it is wrinkled, but do not heavily starch it.

2. Use a 1.6/80 or 2.0/80 twin needle in the machine. Thread the machine with two spools of fine thread (see Perfecting the Pintuck on page 17).

3. Do some test stitching on a scrap of fabric at least 5" square. With the fabric flat, simply sew a straight line with a shortened straight stitch (L = 1.5–2.0), sewing at least 1" from the edge of the fabric. The fabric between the double rows of stitching should form a little ridge (see Perfecting the Pintuck on page 19).

4. When you like the pintucks on the sample, begin sewing the project. Sew the first row, turn the fabric around, and sew another row right next to the first. If you are using a pintuck foot, run the first row of stitching in the outer groove of the foot as you sew the second row.

Stitching the second pintuck row

Without a pintuck foot, run the edge of the presser foot along the first row of stitching right as you sew the second row. For blocks of pintucks, continue adding pintucks to make the necessary fabric width.

Shaped Pintucks

For shaped pintucks, you can practice sewing scallops, as follows:

1. Draw gentle scallops on a scrap of fabric then draw miter lines bisecting the angles. Simply sew right on the line and handle the fabric as if you were straight stitching around a curve.

Sewing pintucked scallops

2. When you reach the miter line, stop with the needle down, lift the presser foot, pivot, put the presser foot back down, and continue stitching.

It looks like the needle will break … it won't. It looks like the fabric will pucker at the corner … it won't. The only time the fabric might pucker is if the angle is very sharp.

Pivoting at the miter lines

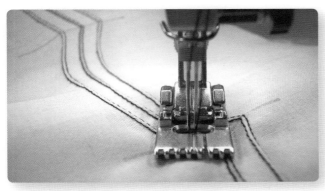

Adding a third row

3. Sew more pintucks alongside the first one. Pivot each row of pintucks at the point where the stitching line crosses the miter line.

Use just a few rows of shaped pintucks to prevent too much distortion – three rows are often best.

4. Soak the fabric to remove markings. Turn the pintucked fabric upside-down on a towel; starch and press.

Corded Pintucks

For corded pintucks, place a soft, heavy thread or cord under the fabric and between the needles. The needles stitch on both sides of the cord, and the zigzag of the bobbin thread sort of couches the cord on the wrong side of the fabric. The cording makes the pintucks more defined and rounder.

Size 12 pearl cotton works well for 1.6/80 needles and a seven-groove foot. Size 8 or 10 works for 2.0/80 needles and a five-groove foot. Some machine throat plates have a small hole just in front of the foot. With these, the ball of pearl cotton can be placed under the front of the

machine, with the cord threaded through the hole and pulled between the needles and behind the foot. Colored pearl cotton can be used to create shadow-colored pintucks.

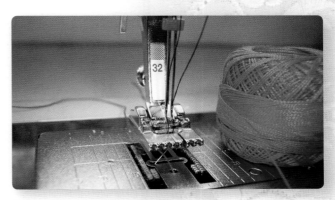

Cording inserted in the throat-plate hole

Perfecting the Pintuck

To thread twin needles, if two spools of thread are not available, wind an extra bobbin and use that instead of a second spool.

On some machines, it is possible to place one thread on either side of the tension disc. If that can be done on your machine, do it. If not, put both threads through the tension disc.

If your machine has two thread guides, above the needle place one thread in each guide. If your machine has only one, place one thread in the guide, and leave the other outside the guide. It is important that the threads be separated above the needle so they don't twist and break.

If your machine has pintuck feet available, use a five-groove or seven-groove pintuck foot. Seven is preferred for very lightweight fabric. If not, use a satin-stitch foot.

If the fabric is too flat, try increasing the needle tension. If the tension must be tightened so much that the thread breaks, try using heavier 50-wt. thread in the bobbin. If the fabric puckers or pulls up too much, so that it forms an actual tuck instead of a

Seven-groove pintuck foot

ridge, loosen the needle tension. If the tensions can't be loosened enough to solve the problem, lightly starch the fabric.

This testing is necessary for every project, because pintucks are dependent on the type and weight of the fabric, the threads and tensions in both needle and bobbin, the grain of the fabric, and the machine used. There is no consistent setting that is always used for pintucks.

There is no way to keep the fabric square in a piece with multiple pintucks. Sewing all the tucks in one direction doesn't seem to make a difference. Just allow for the distortion by using a piece of fabric larger than necessary.

∼ RICKRACK-LACE BRIDGING ∻

Rickrack-lace bridging is an heirloom sewing technique I developed several years ago, which crosses over wonderfully into quilting. Baby rickrack is joined edge to edge as a bridging with insertion or edging lace. Cotton lace and rickrack give the best results.

Preshrink baby cotton rickrack by soaking it in warm water. Hang to dry then press.

Stabilizer and Glue Method

1. Cut strips of water-soluble stabilizer a little wider and longer than needed. Piece the strips together by overlapping the ends and securing them with water-soluble glue.

2. Use a ruler and a blue washout marker to draw a straight line the entire length of the strip.

3. Using water-soluble glue, glue-baste the baby rickrack along the marked line on the stabilizer strip.

4. Glue-baste a piece of lace on one side of the rickrack so that the lace heading touches the rickrack points.

5. Similarly glue-baste a length of lace on the other side of the rickrack. Repeat for as many strips of lace and rickrack as desired. Allow the glue to dry thoroughly.

Sticky-Backed Stabilizer

1. Cut strips of sticky-backed, water-soluble stabilizer as long as and a little narrower than needed.

2. Piece the stabilizer, if necessary, by removing ¼" of the paper backing at one end (do this easily by scoring the paper with a pin) and overlapping another strip by ¼".

3. On the stabilizer side, use a ruler and a blue washout marker to draw a straight line the entire length of the strip.

4. Pin the strip, paper side up, to an ironing board, or tape the strip to a cutting table. Remove the paper, exposing the sticky side of the stabilizer.

5. Without stretching it, stick the baby rickrack along the marked line on the strip.

6. Without stretching it, stick a piece of lace on one side of the rickrack so that the lace heading touches the rickrack points. The lace can be lifted and repositioned as necessary.

7. Similarly, place a length of lace on the other side of the rickrack. Repeat for as many strips of lace and rickrack as desired. Finger-press the lace and rickrack firmly to the stabilizer.

If the lace has a large open weave and the adhesive will drag on the bottom of the presser foot, place a layer of thin, clear, water-soluble stabilizer over the lace and rickrack.

Stitching Rickrack and Lace

1. Using fine cotton thread to match the lace and a zigzag stitch (L = 0.5–0.8, W = 2.0–3.0), sew over the lace heading so that it is encased in the zigzag and the points of the rickrack are caught with one or two stitches at each point.

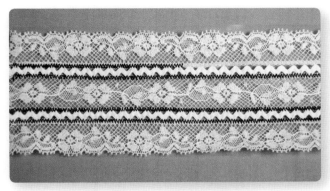

Zigzag stitch the rickrack and lace together.

2. Soak the rickrack-lace piece in water to remove the stabilizer and glue. Roll the piece in a towel to remove excess water then press dry.

3. Stitch the rickrack-lace piece to fabric with a zigzag or pintuck stitch.

❧ CATHEDRAL LACE WINDOWS ❧

This technique creates see-through lace ovals that can be used on garments as well as quilts. Use a lightweight natural-fiber fabric. Cotton batiste is ideal. Handkerchief linen and quilting cottons are also suitable but slightly bulkier.

1. For ⅝"–¾" wide lace, cut two *bias* fabric strips 2½" wide. Place the strips right sides together and machine baste by sewing down the center of the strips with a long straight stitch and loosened needle tension.

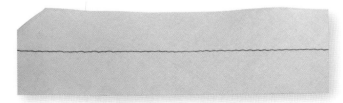

Sew the bias strips together.

Press the strips open.

2. Open the fabric layers and press them as if you were pressing seam allowances open.

Gently pull the seam open. You should be able to see "air" between the large stitches. If not, the seam hasn't been pressed open correctly, and the rest of the steps will not work.

3. Center a strip of insertion cotton lace, right side down, over the seam. Machine-baste through the center of the lace.

Machine-baste the lace along the fabric seam.

4. Open up the fabric strips and zigzag (W = 1.5, L = 1.5) over one heading of the lace, through one layer of fabric only. Repeat for the other heading of the lace. Pull out the basting threads holding the lace in place.

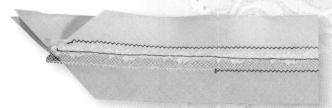

Zigzag stitch a lace header to one layer of fabric, then repeat for the other header.

5. Again, press the strip with the seam pressed open. The lace side of the strip will be the underside of the finished cathedral lace windows strip.

6. On the right side (fabric only) of the strip, make marks along the seam line every 2¼". Using fine thread to match the fabric, stitch a tiny bar tack at each mark, so that both sides of the seam are caught in the stitching.

Sew a bar tack across the seam every 2¼".

7. Remove the basting thread from the center seam. Fold back each bias fabric "lip" between the bar tacks to expose the full width of the insertion lace. Press the lips, one at a time, and secure each lip with pins or a tiny bit of water-soluble glue.

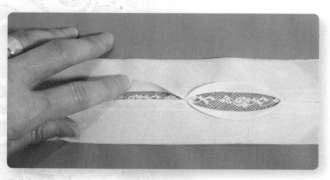

Fold the lips back and pin or glue.

8. Straight-stitch (L = 1.5) very close to the outer folded edges of the lips with matching fine cotton thread or with matching or contrasting rayon, cotton, or silk machine-embroidery thread.

Alternatively, you can stitch the lips with a tiny blind-hem stitch (L = 0.5, W = 1.0) and invisible thread in the needle. The straight part of the stitch goes into the fabric just outside the lips, and the tiny zigzags bite into the lips. Use lightweight tearaway stabilizer under the fabric.

Finished lace windows

9. Trim the raw edges of the strip so that both long edges are the same distance from the center.

10. For inserting the lace window strip into fabric, the two fabric pieces *must* be on the straight grain to stabilize the bias strip. Sew the pieces right sides together and press the seam allowances away from the lace strip.

11. Sew over the seam and seam allowances from the right side with a decorative machine stitch, if desired.

Tip

A pretty option. Satin-stitch a small oval or heart on both sides of each bar tack between the lace windows.

Laces of different widths. You need to change the width of the bias strips and the spacing between the bar tacks for laces of different widths. For example, for 1" wide insertion lace, use 3" wide bias strips, and stitch the bar tacks 2½" apart.

∼ SHAPED BIAS STRIPS ∽

Bias strips from lightweight, loosely woven fabrics with a lot of bias stretch, like handkerchief linen and some quilting cottons, are best for this technique. For an heirloom look, use 100 percent cotton batiste for the base fabric, especially if you are using a pin stitch.

1. Starch and press the batiste base fabric. Use a blue washout marker to trace the design onto the batiste.

2. Use a rotary cutter and ruler to cut handkerchief linen or cotton into scant 1⅛" wide bias strips. If necessary, sew the bias strips together, end to end with diagonal seams.

3. Use a ½" (12 mm) bias-tape maker to press under the edges of the bias strips.

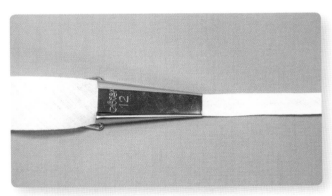

Using a bias-tape maker

4. Shape the pressed bias strips along the traced lines, using pins or water-soluble glue to hold them in place. Begin a strip where the raw end will be caught in a seam line, hidden under an appliqué piece, or covered by an overlying strip. If using glue, do not glue the intersections.

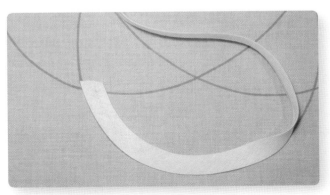

Shaping a bias strip

To miter the angles, follow the steps for Lace Shaping on page 13.

5. If the strip is not long enough for an entire interlaced design, cut the strip so that the end will be hidden under an intersection, and begin another strip at the same place, overlapping the ends by ½".

6. After shaping a complete interlaced design, the crossing direction of some of the intersections can be changed, if necessary. Cut the top strip and tuck the ends under the other strip. Obviously, this cannot be done when the strip underneath has already been cut, so some planning is required.

7. Stitch both sides of the strips with fine thread, a 100 or 110 universal or topstitch needle, and a tiny pin stitch (L = 2.0–2.5, W = 1.5–2.0), catching the bias strips with just the side-to-side portions of the stitch. Do not trim the fabric away behind the bias strips as would be done with lace strips.

Alternately, use a tiny zigzag or blind stitch with a small needle and fine matching thread or invisible thread. Stitch only along the overlapping strip at the intersections to retain the interlaced look.

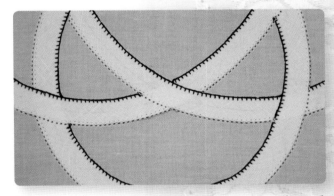

Pinstitched with contrasting thread on the outer edge and matching thread on the inner edge.

∼ SEMINOLE LACEWORK ∽

I was inspired by simple strip-pieced Seminole patchwork when I developed this technique. It is made heirloom-like by substituting insertion lace for the seams.

1. From fabric A, cut a strip 2⅜" wide. From fabric B, cut two strips 2¾" wide.

2. With all the pieces right side up, place an insertion lace along both long edges of the fabric-A strip so that half the width of the lace covers the edges of the fabric.

3. Zigzag (L = 0.5–0.8, W = 2.5) over the lace headers with fine cotton thread and a size 70 needle.

Add lace edges to the fabric-A strip.

4. Place the fabric-B strips on each side of fabric A so the fabrics just meet under the center of the lace. Zigzag as before.

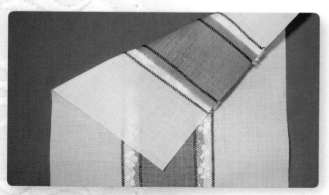

Fabrics A and B meet under the lace.

5. Trim away the fabric under the lace, close to the stitching.

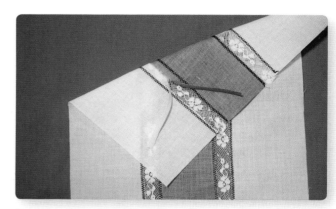

Trim fabrics A and B.

6. Press the fabric-lace strip. From it, cut 2⅜" segments perpendicular to the rows of lace.

7. Positioning the lace over the fabric as before, sew the lace to one side of each segment.

Add lace to each segment.

8. Sew the segments together, offsetting the fabrics in Seminole fashion. The raw segment edges should meet under the lace strips.

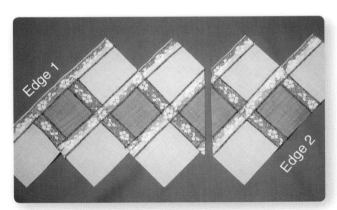

Offset the segments.

9. To square the ends of the completed Seminole strip, make a cut across the center of one of the fabric-A squares.

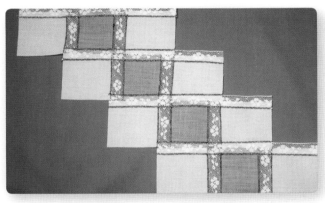

Cut through a fabric-A square.

10. Join the two resulting pieces by sewing edge 1 to edge 2 (remember to offset the squares). Trim the fabric from behind the lace.

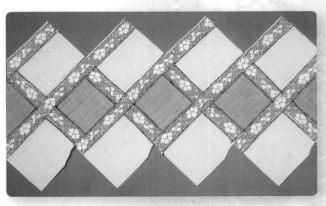

Trim the fabric under the lace.

11. Draw lines on the long edges of the Seminole strip about ¼" outside the points of the fabric-A squares.

12. Place the header of insertion or edging lace on the drawn lines and zigzag the inner edge of the lace. Trim the fabric from behind the lace.

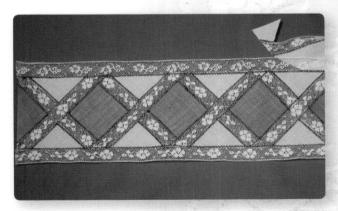

Trim the fabric from under the lace.

13. Stitch the Seminole lacework strip on top of another fabric, or stitch the outer borders of the lace to batiste blocks.

The Seminole strips can be wider or narrower as long as you cut the outer strips ⅜" wider than the center strips. Cut the segments the same width as the center strips.

~ SHAPED PUFFING ~

Puffing is simply a strip of fabric gathered along both long edges. The puffed strip is then shaped and sewn to a base fabric, and lace or trim is used to cover the raw edges. In heirloom sewing, this puffed fabric is usually cotton batiste.

1. Starch and press the base fabric. With a washout marker, draw placement lines for the innermost and outermost lace edges.

2. For the puffing, cut or tear fabric strips about ½" narrower than the space between the placement lines on the base fabric. To allow for fullness, the puffing strip needs to be one and a half to two times the desired finished length. Press the strips but do not starch them.

If necessary to achieve the desired length for the puffing, you can join fabric strips end to end.

3. Gather the puffing strip along both long edges, as follows:

For short or narrow strips, you will need two rows of straight stitches, sewn ¼" and ½" from both edges. Stitch (L = 2.5–3.0) the rows on the wrong side of the strip with a loosened needle tension and polyester or cotton-covered polyester thread in the bobbin. Pull up all four bobbin threads at once to gather the strip.

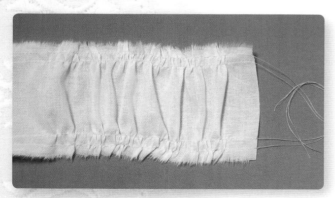

Gathering the puffing strip

For longer strips, try using a gathering foot. Stitch length and tension may both need to be adjusted to create even, not-too-tight gathers. Sew, with the fabric right side up, ⅜" from the raw edges. Gather one side of the strip then the other side. Strips narrower than 2½" or 3" can be difficult to maneuver under the gathering foot.

4. Shape the puffed strip between the marked lines on the base fabric. The raw edges of the strip should be about ¼" inside the lines. Pin or glue the strip to the base fabric.

5. Adjust the gathers so they are all perpendicular to the drawn lines by pulling up the bobbin threads on the right side of the fabric. If a gathering foot was used and the gathers are held firmly in place, simply ease the gathers with your fingers and glue or pin them well.

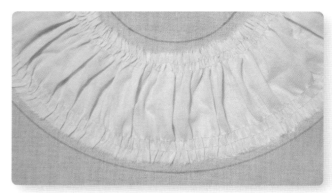

Puffed strip positioned on base fabric

6. Press the puffing seam allowances flat. Shape lace along both edges of the puffing so that the outer headers of the insertion lace strips are along the drawn lines (see Lace Shaping, page 13).

Adding lace to the puffing

7. Zigzag (L = 0.5–0.8, W = 2.0–2.5) along both headers of both lace strips through all the layers of fabric.

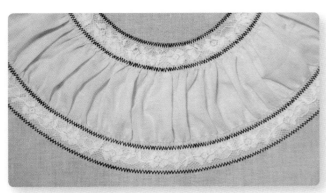

Zigzag the headers.

Pin stitches may be used along the outer headers of the lace strips (those edges not covering the puffing), but in most cases, it is preferable to zigzag the edges of lace along the puffing, because the gathers can get bulky.

8. Soak the piece in water to remove the markings and glue, if used. Allow to air dry, then lightly starch and press the fabric and lace outside the puffing. Avoid pressing the puffing, although there is no way to prevent it from wrinkling and becoming somewhat flat.

9. On the wrong side, trim away the base fabric behind the puffing. Behind the laces, trim away the base fabric and the puffing seam allowances. A tiny bit of base fabric will remain in the stitching. Remove any visible gathering threads.

Trim the fabric from behind the puffing and lace.

∿ REVERSE-APPLIQUÉ WINDOWS ❧

This technique features a unique look for reverse appliqué by using sheer fabric to create windows. The reverse appliqué is made with facings of water-soluble stabilizer.

1. Starch the fabrics well and press dry to help stabilize them. Using a blue washout pen, trace the design onto batiste.

2. Cut the stabilizer at least ½" larger than the motif. Pin the stabilizer to the right side of the fabric over the motif.

Place stabilizer over the motif.

3. With a short straight stitch (L = 1.5), sew around the motif on the drawn line. At acute angles, take one tiny stitch across the point.

Sew around the motif.

4. Cut the fabric and the stabilizer from inside the stitched shape, leaving a ⅛" seam allowance. With small, very sharp scissors, clip the curves and points all the way to, but not through, the stitching line.

Cut out the center and clip the seam allowance.

5. Turn the stabilizer to the wrong side through the center of the motif. Roll the edges to make sure the stitching line is right along the faced edge. Finger-press the edges.
  Because this is water-soluble *stabilizer, be sure not to moisten your fingers for this task!*

Turn the stabilizer to the back.

6. If the stabilizer can be pressed with a pressing cloth without shrinking (test a sample first), press the piece from the fabric side. Do not touch the stabilizer with the iron.

7. Place organza or organdy under the hole, aligning the fabric grain lines in both pieces. Pin. Sew around the appliqué edge with very fine cotton thread, a 70 universal needle, and a tiny blindstitch (L = 0.5, W = 1.0–1.5) or a small zigzag (L = 1.0–1.5, W = 1.0–1.5).

If your machine has a pin stitch, use this hallmark stitch of heirloom machine sewing. Use a 100 or 110 universal needle, with L = 2.0–2.5 and W = 1.5–2.0. Stitch so that the forward-and-backward portion of the stitch is in the organza only, and the side-to-side portion bites into the batiste. The large needle, repetitive stitch, and fine thread combine to form a series of tiny holes along the stitching line. The water-soluble stabilizer should provide enough stability so that no other stabilizer is usually necessary. If there are problems with puckering, you can use additional stabilizer under the batiste.

Edge sewn with the pin stitch

8. For added stability, an optional second row of stitching, such as pin stitching with the teeth pointing in toward the motif, a tiny feather stitch, or other decorative stitch, can be sewn a scant ¼" outside the first stitching.

Second row of stitching added

9. On the wrong side, trim away the excess organza. Soak the piece in water to remove the stabilizer and marks.

~ TURNED-EDGE APPLIQUÉ ~

The following two methods work well for simple, large shapes. Freezer-paper templates stabilize the fabric for stitching.

Water-Soluble Facing
1. Starch the fabrics well and press dry to help stabilize them.
2. Trace a reversed appliqué pattern onto freezer paper and cut it out. Iron the freezer paper onto the wrong side of the appliqué fabric. Also trace the pattern onto the batiste base layer as a positioning guide for the appliqué.
3. Place water-soluble stabilizer on the right side of the appliqué fabric. From the wrong side, use a short straight stitch (L = 1.5–2.0) to sew through the fabric and the stabilizer along the freezer-paper edge, all the way around the enclosed shape. Take one stitch across any points.

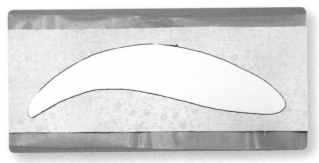
Sew around the shape.

If the appliqué has an edge that will be tucked under another appliqué piece or caught in a seam, do not stitch along that edge.
4. Remove the freezer-paper template, which can be used again. Trim away the fabric and stabilizer outside the stitching line, leaving a ⅛" seam allowance. Clip the curves.

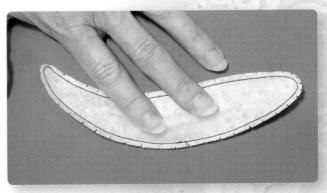
Clip the seam allowance and cut a slit in the stabilizer.

5. For enclosed appliqué shapes, cut a slit in the stabilizer. Carefully turn the appliqué right side out through the slit or an unstitched edge. Make sure the stitching line is right along the faced edge and the points are pushed out as much as possible.

Turn the shape right side out.

Sometimes, especially with small appliqués, the stabilizer will tear to the seam allowance. Just ignore the tear. As long as the seam allowance is turned under, there should be no problem sewing the appliqué to the base fabric, and the stabilizer will wash away.
6. If the stabilizer will allow it, press the appliqué from the fabric side. Some stabilizers will shrink from the heat, so test a sample first and avoid touching the stabilizer directly with the iron.

7. Pin the appliqué to the batiste where indicated by the guideline. Sew the appliqué to the base fabric with a pin stitch. Use fine cotton thread and a 100 or 110 universal needle, with L = 2.0–2.5 and W = 1.5–2.0.

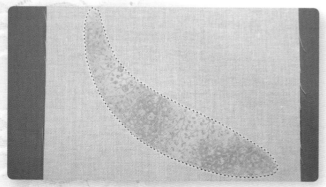

Pin-stitched appliqué

Sew the forward-and-backward portion of the stitch in the batiste only and the side-to-side portion in the appliqué. The large needle, repetitive stitch, and fine thread combine to form a series of very tiny holes along the stitching line.

If your machine does not have a pin stitch, use fine thread, a 70 universal needle, and a tiny blind-hem stitch (L = 0.5, W = 1.0–1.5) or a small zigzag (L = 1.0–1.5, W = 1.0–1.5). Do not cut the batiste away from behind the appliqué.

8. Soak the fabric to remove all traces of stabilizer. Gently squeeze the fabric then roll it in a towel to remove excess water. Lay the fabric flat to air dry, then lightly starch and press.

Water-Soluble Thread

For closed shapes, a scrap of fabric is used in place of the water-soluble stabilizer. For shapes that are not closed, with an opening along the edge that is large enough to turn the piece right side out, two mirror-image appliqués can be prepared at the same time (see the Mirror-image Appliqués tip on page 31). I prefer YLI Wash-A-Way™ Water-Soluble Basting Thread for this technique.

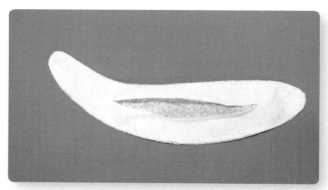

Cutting a slit in the scrap fabric

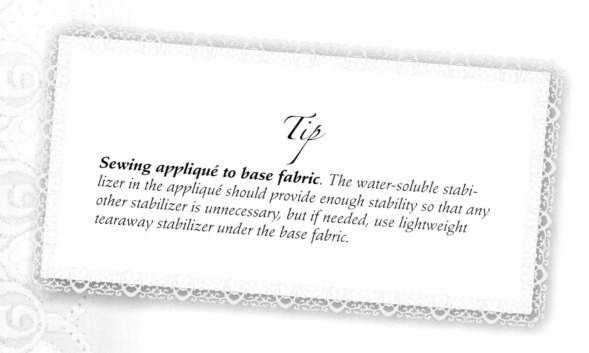

Tip

Sewing appliqué to base fabric. The water-soluble stabilizer in the appliqué should provide enough stability so that any other stabilizer is unnecessary, but if needed, use lightweight tearaway stabilizer under the base fabric.

1. Follow steps 1–4 for Water-Soluble Facing (page 29), but use scrap fabric instead of the stabilizer, and use water-soluble thread in the needle and/or bobbin.

2. Cut a slit in the scrap fabric. Carefully turn the appliqué right side out through the slit or an unstitched edge. Make sure the stitching line is right along the faced edge and the points are pushed out as much as possible. Press the piece firmly.

3. Heavily spray-starch the appliqué, especially along the edges. Press until completely dry. Use a lightweight press cloth to prevent the iron from sticking, and do not move the appliqué until it is completely dry.

4. Gently pull the appliqué and scrap fabric apart along the seam line. The fabrics should separate easily. If they do not, repeat the starch and press steps. Discard the scrap fabric.

Pulling the scrap fabric off the appliqué

5. Sew the appliqué to the base fabric as described in steps 7 and 8 for Water-Soluble Facing, page 30.

Mirror-image appliqués

Tip

Mirror-image appliqués. For designs that are not closed shapes, scrap fabric is not necessary. You can prepare two mirror-image appliqués at the same time. Use water-soluble thread to sew two layers of appliqué fabric right sides together, leaving a section unstitched for turning. Trim, turn, press, starch, press, then separate the two appliqués.

❧ NETTING INSERTIONS ❧

In this technique, English cotton netting is embellished with decorative machine stitches and used to form lace-like inserts in cotton batiste. Synthetic tulle can be used instead of cotton netting. It is much less expensive but not as soft.

1. Preshrink the cotton netting by soaking it in warm water and air-drying it. It will shrink 25 percent or more in width.

2. Starch and press the batiste fabric and cotton netting. (Do not press synthetic tulle, if used.)

Six-inch squares before and after shrinking

3. Cut one or two layers of heavyweight water-soluble stabilizer, depending on the weight of the stabilizer and the humidity. High humidity makes some stabilizers soft and limp, so multiple layers may be required.

4. Heavily trace the insertion stitching lines onto the batiste with a blue washout marker.

5. With all pieces right side up, place the stabilizer over the batiste and the netting over the stabilizer; pin. If the lines are difficult to see, retrace them on the netting.

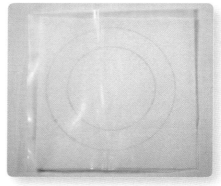

Layer the batiste, stabilizer, and netting.

6. Choose a satin stitch (W = 3.5). Use a size 80 needle and 50 wt. cotton thread or machine embroidery thread to match the netting.

Alternatively, you can use an entredeux stitch (W = 3.5, L = 3.0) if your machine has it. Use lightweight cotton thread, to match the netting, in needle and bobbin. Use a 100 or 110 universal or 100 wing needle.

7. Stitch along all marked lines through the netting, stabilizer, and batiste.

Stitch on the lines.

8. On the wrong side, with small, sharp, blunt-tipped scissors, trim away the batiste only between the parallel stitching lines. Cut very close to the stitching without cutting the stabilizer.

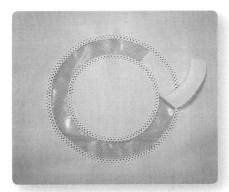

Cut away only the batiste.

9. Using a size 80 universal or embroidery needle and 50-wt. cotton thread or 40-wt. machine embroidery thread to match the netting, sew a decorative stitch between the entredeux- or satin-stitched lines, through the netting and stabilizer.

Choose a stitch that is lacy looking and somewhat open instead of a satin fill stitch. Also, a short pattern rather than a long one is easiest to use. I like using a snowflake-type stitch.

Use an embroidery stitch on top of the netting.

10. On the right side, trim away the netting and stabilizer from over the batiste, everywhere except between the parallel lines of stitching. Trim very close to the stitching. If it's easier, trim only the netting and leave the stabilizer.

Trim away the netting and stabilizer.

11. Soak the piece in plain, clear water to remove all of the stabilizer and markings. Roll the piece in a towel to remove excess water but do not wring. Air-dry or iron dry. Starch and press again.

Designed, sewn, and quilted by the author ❧ *36" x 43"*

Beginning Heirloom
Baby Quilt

BEGINNING HEIRLOOM BABY QUILT

If you've never done heirloom machine sewing, this is the
perfect first project. You can learn some basic techniques
while making this baby quilt. The heirloom sewing is done
on cotton batiste, which is then layered over your choice
of fabric, which shadows through the semi-sheer batiste.
Decorative machine stitching accents the heirloom sewing.

 Techniques

Supplies

Threads
- Fine cotton to match lace
- 50-wt. cotton, to blend with colored fabrics
- Machine embroidery, to coordinate with fabrics

Machine Needles
- 65 or 70 universal
- 80 universal
- 1.6/80 or 2.0/80 twin

Project Supplies
- 5- or 7-groove pintuck foot, if available for machine
- Blue washout marker
- Water-soluble stabilizer
- Small, sharp, preferably round-tipped scissors

Fabrics
Yardages are based on a useable width of at least 40"
- White cotton batiste 1¾ yd.
- Pink solid 1¾ yd.
- Pink small print ¾ yd.
- 2½" wide embroidered cotton eyelet insertion ¾ yd.
- ⅝" wide white beading lace 1⅓ yd.
- ⅝" wide white insertion lace 5⅓ yd.
- ⅛" wide satin ribbon 1⅓ yd.
- Backing 1⅜ yd.
- Batting 40" x 47"

Cutting

Cut strips selvage to selvage.

White cotton batiste
- 1 rectangle 16" x 23" (A)
- 2 strips 9" x 23" (B)
- 2 strips 3" x 23" B shadow
- 2 strips 9" x 16" (C)
- 2 strips 3" x 16" C shadow
- 4 squares 8½" (D)
- 4 squares 3" D shadow

Pink solid
- 1 rectangle 14½" x 21½" (A)
- 2 strips 7½" x 21½" (B)
- 2 strips 7½" x 14½" (C)
- 4 squares 7½" (D)
- 4 strips 2¼" for binding

Pink small print
- Eight 2½" strips for sashing and borders

Center Panel

1. Stitch 1⅓ yd. beading lace to 1⅓ yd. insertion lace, using the joining lace to lace technique. Press. Cut the resulting beading-insertion strip in half to make two lengths about 24".

2. Cut the embroidered cotton eyelet strip to the same length as the beading-insertion strips. Use the joining lace to fabric (roll and whip) technique to sew the beading-insertion strips to both long edges of the eyelet strip. Press.

3. Fold batiste rectangle A in half lengthwise and finger-press the fold. Center the beading-insertion-eyelet strip on the fold.

4. Stitch the outer edges of the strip to the batiste by using the joining lace to fabric technique (three-step method).

5. With a blue washout marker, draw lines 1" outside both long edges of the beading-insertion-eyelet strips, as in the illustration.

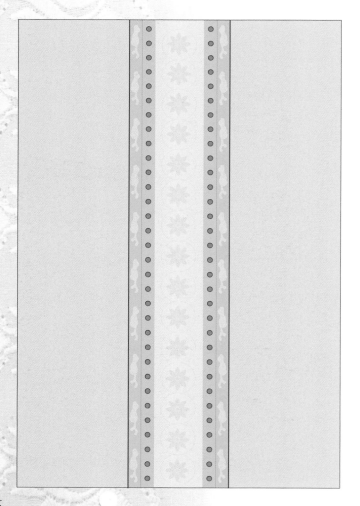

1. embroidered eyelet
2. beading lace with ribbon
3. insertion lace
4. 1 row decorative stitches
5. 3 rows decorative stitches

6. Cut two insertion lace strips the length of rectangle A. Pin the inner edges of the strips along the drawn lines. Use the joining lace to fabric technique (three-step method) to stitch the lace insertion to the batiste.

7. With machine embroidery thread, a size 80 needle, and water-soluble stabilizer under the fabric, sew a decorative stitch on the batiste between the laces.

I used a small floral vine stitch between the laces in my quilt.

8. Stitch one or more rows of another decorative stitch outside the rows of lace.

I used three rows of a tiny feather or briar stitch.

9. Soak the panel in water to remove the water-soluble stabilizer and blue marks. Air dry. Spray starch and press.

10. Use a bodkin or small safety pin to weave ⅛" satin ribbon through the holes in the beading. Trim the A panel to 14½" x 21½". Layer the panel over pink solid rectangle A. Pin the pieces together and treat as one from here on.

Corner Heart Squares

1. Fold the batiste D corner squares in quarters diagonally and finger-press the folds.

2. Trace the large and small hearts from template 1 (page 92) onto the squares, aligning the fold lines with the appropriate lines on the template.

3. Use the lace shaping technique to sew the insertion lace around the large lace hearts.

4. Use the shadow appliqué technique and the 3" batiste squares (D shadow) to stitch the small hearts. Trim away the excess appliqué fabric outside the stitching.

5. Soak the squares in warm water to remove the blue markings. Air dry. Spray starch and press.

6. Trim the squares to 7½". Layer the squares over the pink D squares and treat as one.

Tip

To prevent the ribbon from catching and pulling up in loops, stitch by hand or machine through all the layers at the places where the ribbon weaves underneath the beading.

Scallop Borders

1. Trace template 2 (page 93) onto batiste strips B and C, repeating the scallops for the full length of the strips.

2. Place the batiste B and C strips over their corresponding batiste shadow strips, aligning their raw edges as shown on the template. Stitch using the shadow appliqué technique. Trim away the excess shadow fabric outside the shadow area, close to the stitching.

3. For each B and C strip, stitch a twin-needle pintuck along the pintuck line. Stitch two more pintucks, one on each side of the first one.

4. Soak the panels in warm water to remove the blue markings. Air dry. Spray starch and press.

5. With the cut edge on the shadow appliqué side 2½" beyond the tops of the scallops, trim the B strips to 7½" x 21½" and trim the C strips to 7½" x 14½".

6. Layer a batiste B strip over a B pink solid strip. Pin together and treat as one panel from here on. Repeat for the remaining B strip and the C strips.

∾ QUILT ASSEMBLY ∾

1. Sew sashing strips to the long sides of panel A. Trim the sashing even with the raw edges of A.

2. Add the B panels to the sides of panel A with the shadowed scallops next to A.

3. Sew sashing strips to the short sides of the C panels. Trim. Join the corner heart squares to the C panels so that all the hearts will point toward the center of the quilt.

4. Sew sashing to the top and bottom of the A–B panels, then add the C panels to the top and bottom.

5. Sew border strips to the sides of the quilt, then along the top and bottom. Trim.

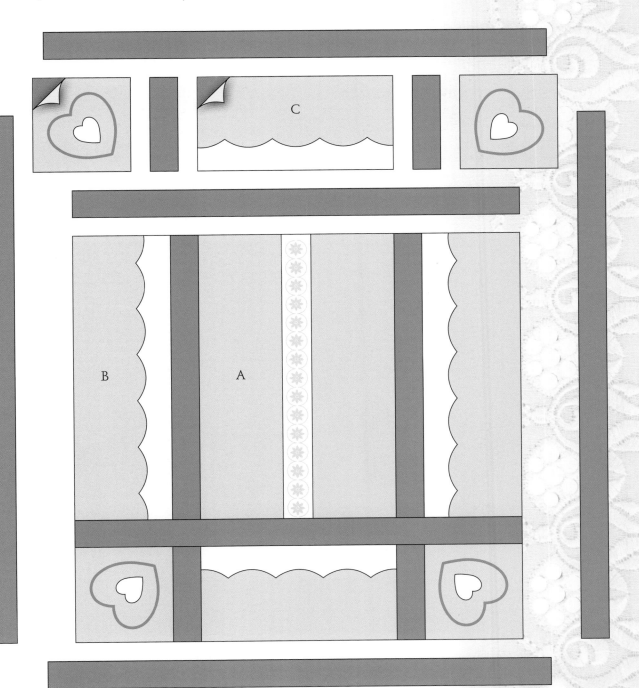

Suggested Quilting

Layer the backing, batting, and quilt top; baste. With invisible thread, stitch in the ditch of the sashing seam lines. Stitch along the lace zigzag stitching, shadow appliqué stitching, outer rows of pintucks, and all decorative stitching.

With matching thread, stitch ¼" outside the shadow appliqué hearts and ¼" outside the shadow appliqué scallop stitching, adding loops at the peaks of the scallops. Stitch scallops halfway between the shadow appliqué scallops and the pintucks. Stitch scallops ½" outside the pintucks, with three loops at the peaks of scallops. Stitch a three-loop motif above the hearts. Stitch around the motifs in the embroidered eyelet insertion. Stitch a cabled border outside the decorative stitching in the center panel and sashing.

Add binding to finish the raw edges of the quilt.

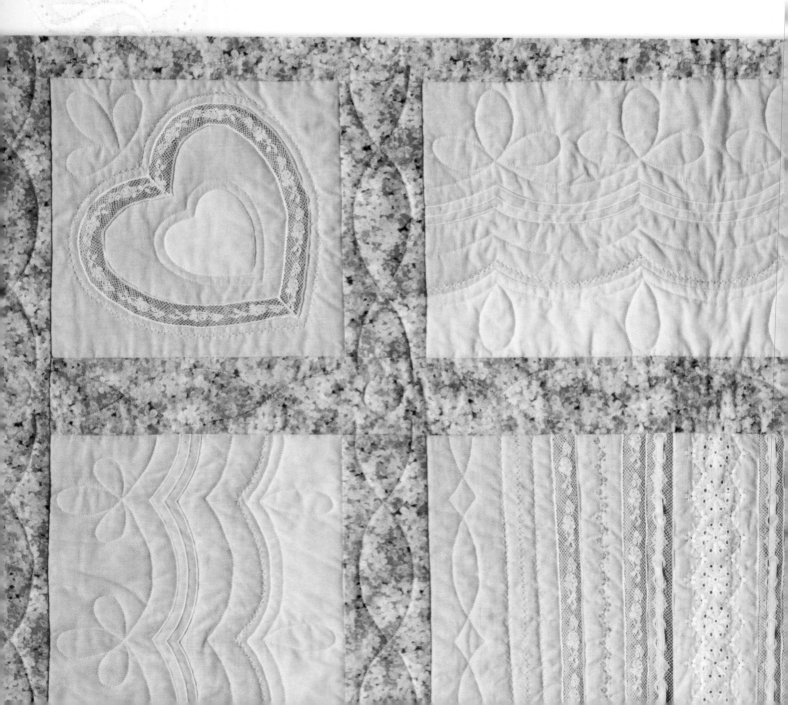

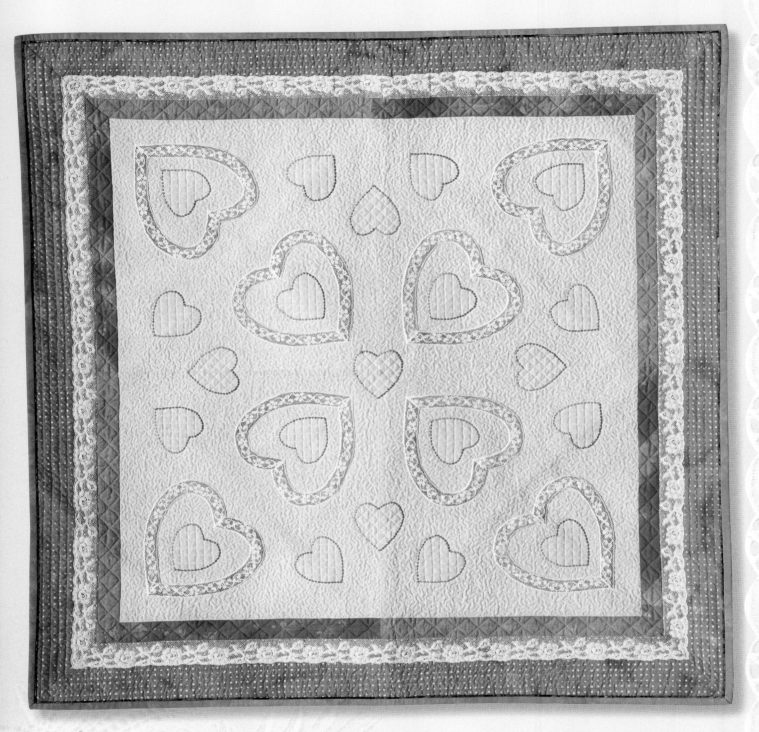

Designed, sewn, and quilted by the author ✤ *32" x 32"*

Hot Lace ♡ Hearts

HOT LACE HEARTS

White shaped-lace hearts on white batiste are layered over a pieced background of hot pink and bright orange. Decorative machine stitches in pink and orange form the smaller hearts. The inner border is a pink, orange, and gray batik, with gray piping and lace, followed by an orange outer border.

Techniques
Lace Shaping   page 13

Supplies
Threads
- Fine white cotton
- Machine embroidery, to match pink and orange fabrics
- 50-wt. cotton, to blend with fabrics for piecing
- Desired quilting threads

Machine Needles
- 70 and 80

Project Supplies
- Lightweight tearaway stabilizer.

Fabrics
Yardages are based on a useable width of at least 40"
- White cotton batiste 1 yd.
- Hot pink ⅔ yd. for background and inner border
- Hot orange 1 yd. for background, inner border, and binding
- Orange, pink, and gray batik ⅝ yd.
- Gray ¼ yd. for piping
- ⅝" wide white insertion lace 5¼ yd.
- 1¼" wide white edging lace 4 yd.
- Tiny piping cord 4 yd.
- Backing 1⅛ yd.
- Batting 36" x 36"

Cutting
Cut strips selvage to selvage.
White cotton batiste
- 4 squares   14"

Hot Pink
- 2 squares   13¼", cut in quarters diagonally for background
- 4 strips   1½" x 18" for inner border

Hot Orange
- 2 squares   13¼", cut in quarters diagonally for background
- 4 strips   1½" x 18" for inner border
- 4 strips   2¼" for binding

Orange, pink, and gray batik
- 4 strips   3½" x 35½" for outer border

Gray
- 4 strips   1" for piping

Block Embellishments

1. Fold the 14" batiste squares in quarters diagonally and finger press the folds. Open the squares and trace two of the large heart templates (page 92) in each square, as shown in the figure. Use the dashed line labeled "diagonal center of block for Hot Lace Hearts" to position the hearts in the squares.

2. Follow the lace shaping technique to shape, stitch, and trim the lace hearts. Trim the batiste squares to 12½", with the hearts centered.

3. Sew two hot pink triangles and two hot orange triangles together to make a 12½" square, matching colors on opposite sides of the block. Make four background squares like this.

4. Layer the batiste squares over the background squares so that a pink triangle is under the right-hand side of every heart. Pin the layers together and treat as one from here on.

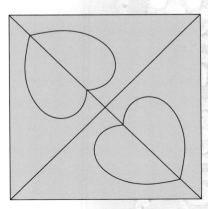

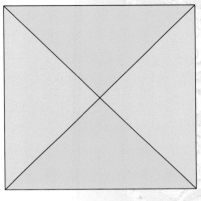

Quilt Assembly

1. Sew the blocks together so the hearts point toward the center and the corners, as shown in the quilt assembly diagram.

2. Trace the small heart, from template on page 92, in the center of each lace heart and in the center of the quilt top. Trace template 3 (page 94) and center it over the four block seam lines, as in the quilt photo.

3. Position lightweight tearaway stabilizer under the fabric and sew a small decorative stitch around all the small hearts with machine embroidery thread. Use orange thread over the orange fabric and pink thread over the pink fabric.

I used small satin-stitch dots to outline the hearts in my quilt.

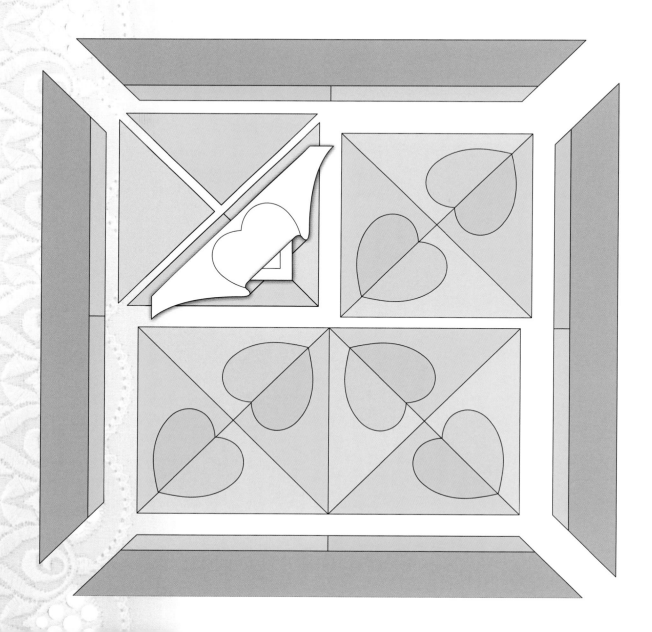

Borders

1. For the inner border, join the short ends of one pink and one orange strip. Make four combined strips like this.

2. Cut the edging lace the same length as the outer border strips. Lay a lace strip on the right side of the outer border strips, with the straight edge of the lace ⅛" from the raw edge of each border strip. Sew the lace header to the border strips.

3. Then use fine white thread and a small zigzag stitch to sew the lace's scalloped edge to the border strips.

4. Arrange the inner border strips around the quilt so that the pink and orange fabrics will correspond to the background fabrics in the blocks. Then sew the lace-edged outer border strips to the inner border strips with a ¼" seam allowance.

The lace headers will be enclosed in the border seams.

5. Pin and sew all four border strips to the quilt top and miter the corners.

Suggested Quilting

Layer the backing, batting, and quilt top; baste. Use invisible thread to stitch in the ditch along all lace-fabric seams and around the decorative-stitched hearts.

Use white #100 silk thread to crosshatch inside the small hearts, stipple in the remaining batiste areas, and stitch along the scallops and motifs within the lace border.

Use pink and orange machine embroidery thread to stitch diamonds in the pink and orange borders and to channel quilt the batik border.

Sew the gray strips together, end to end, for piping. Cover the narrow cord with the gray strip. Trim the seam allowance to ¼". Sew the piping to the quilt.

Add binding to finish the raw edges of the quilt.

Designed, sewn, and quilted by the author ❧ 40" x 47"

Cathedral Lace Window
Baby Quilt

CATHEDRAL LACE WINDOW BABY QUILT

Techniques
Cathedral Lace Windows   page 21

Supplies
Threads
- Machine embroidery, to match blue and green fabrics
- Invisible thread
- Ivory sewing thread
- Desired quilting thread

Project Supplies
- Water-soluble glue or glue stick

Fabrics
Yardages are based on a useable width of at least 40"
- Ivory cotton batiste 1¾ yd.
- Green lengthwise stripe ⅝ yd.
- Blue lengthwise stripe 1⅓ yd.
- Green solid ¾ yd.
- Blue solid ⅝ yd.
- Ivory ½ yd.
- ⅝" wide ivory insertion lace 8 yd.
- Backing 2⅞ yd.
- Batting 48" x 55"

Cutting
Cut strips selvage to selvage, unless lengthwise strips are indicated.

Ivory cotton batiste
- 60 bias strips 2½" x 9" with squared, not angled, ends

Green stripe
- 2 strips   7½"; from these cut
  - 30 strips 2½" x 7½"

Blue stripe
- 2 strips   7½"; from these cut
  - 30 strips 2½ x 7½"
- Bias strips   2¼" for binding

Green solid
- 6 strips   1"; from these cut
  - 30 strips 1" x 7½"
- 1 strip   7½"; from this cut
  - 15 rectangles 2½" x 7½" for underlay
- 5 strips   1" for border

Blue Solid
- 6 strips   1"; from these cut
  - 30 strips 1" x 7½"
- 1 strip   7½"; from this cut
  - 15 strips 2½" x 7½" for underlay

Ivory
- 5 strips   2½" for border

Cathedral Lace Window Strips

1. Follow steps 1–5 of the cathedral lace windows technique.

2. In step 6, make four marks on each pair of strips, centering the marks along the length of the strip.

3. Follow step 7 to remove the basting threads and fold back the lips.

4. Use a blind-hem stitch (L = 0.5, W = 1.0) and invisible thread to stitch the folded edges of the lips.

5. If desired, satin stitch small ovals or hearts between the lace windows.

6. Make 15 cathedral window strips with blue embroidery and 15 strips with green embroidery.

7. Trim the strips so that both edges are 1¼" from the center line of the strip, making the strips 2½" wide.

8. Cut the strips to 7½" in length, centering the windows.

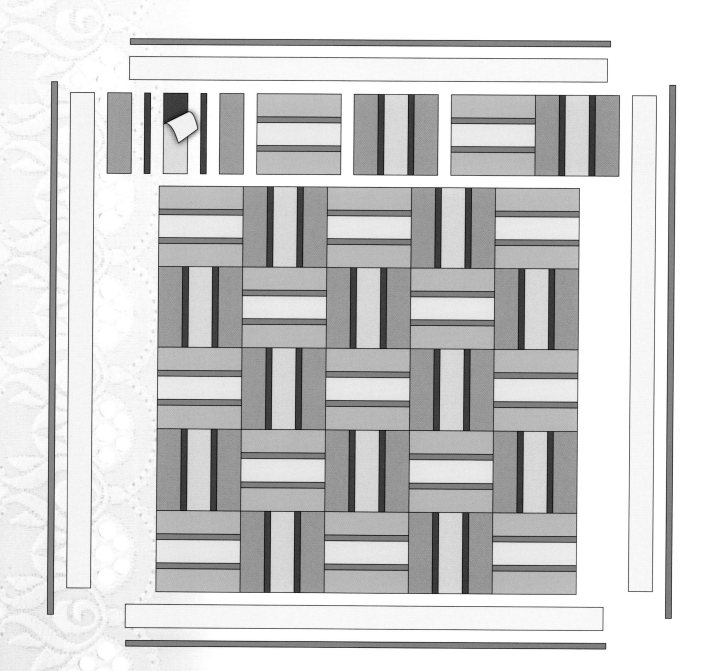

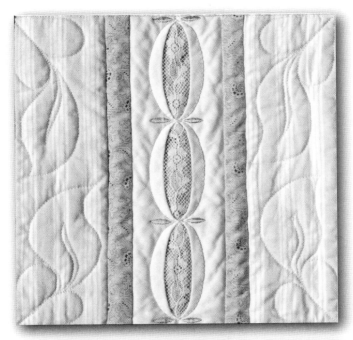

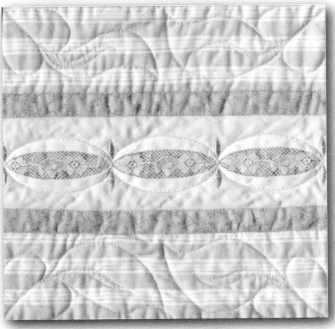

9. Place 15 window strips over green underlay rectangles, and 15 window strips over blue underlay rectangles, all right side up. Pin together and treat the two layers as one from here on.

Quilt Assembly (see facing page)

1. Sew a 1" green strip to one side of every 2½" green stripe strip. Sew a 1" blue strip to one side of every 2½" blue stripe strip. Press.

2. Sew the pieces from step 1 to both sides of a window strip of the same color, with the solid-color strip next to the window strip.

3. Sew the blocks together into six rows of five each, alternating the color and direction of the strips. Sew the rows together.

4. Cut one of the ivory border strips in half and sew a half strip to two of the remaining border strips. Sew these strips to the sides of the quilt. Trim any excess length. Sew ivory border strips to the top and bottom of the quilt. Trim.

5. Sew the five green border strips together, end to end, with diagonal seams. From this strip, cut the lengths needed to sew green border strips to the sides of the quilt and then the top and bottom.

Suggested Quilting

Layer the backing, batting, and quilt top; baste. With invisible or fine ivory thread, stitch in the ditch of all seams. Stitch along the windows, just next to the lips.

With ivory thread, quilt a cable pattern in the stripes in the blocks and in the ivory border.

Add binding to finish the raw edges of the quilt.

Designed, sewn, and quilted by the author ❧ *50" x 50"*

Violet Heirloom

VIOLET HEIRLOOM

Ivory cotton batiste is embellished with ivory interlaced shaped lace, shaped bias linen strips, and a turned-edge appliqué motif. The design is accentuated when layered over a medium violet fabric. Small blocks around the central motif display rickrack-lace bridging strips and Seminole lacework strips. VIOLET HEIRLOOM was quilted with invisible thread, along with ivory and violet rayon machine embroidery thread.

Techniques

Lace Shaping	page 13
Rickrack-Lace Bridging	page 20
Shaped Bias Strips	page 23
Seminole Lacework	page 23
Turned-Edge Appliqué	page 29

Supplies

Threads
- Fine ivory cotton
- Ivory piecing thread
- Desired quilting threads

Machine Needles
- 70, 80, and 100 or 110 universal or topstitch

Project Supplies
- Water-soluble stabilizer
- Water-soluble glue or glue stick
- Blue washout marker
- ½" bias tape maker

Fabrics
Yardages are based on a useable width of at least 40"
- Ivory cotton batiste 1 yd.
- Violet 2⅛ yd.
- Small floral (violet on ivory) 1 yd.
- Large floral (violet on ivory) 1⅛ yd.
- Ivory handkerchief linen or quilt-weight cotton ½ yd.
- ⅝" wide ivory edging lace 5½ yd.
- ⅝" wide ivory insertion lace 10½ yd.
- ¼" wide ivory cotton rickrack 3⅔ yd.
- Backing 3⅜ yd.
- Batting 58" x 58"

Cutting
Cut strips selvage to selvage.

Ivory cotton batiste
- 2 squares   13" for corner triangles (A) (Do not separate triangles yet.)
- 1 square   18" for quilt center

Violet
- 1 square   16½" for quilt center
- 2 squares   13", cut in half diagonally (A)
- 2 strips   6½"; from these cut
  - 8 rectangles 3¼" x 6½" (B)
  - 4 rectangles 5½" x 6½" (C)
- 14 strips   1" for accent borders
- 6 strips   3¼" for ½" binding

Small floral (violet on ivory)
- 2 strips   6½"; from these cut
  - 8 rectangles 3¾" x 6½" (D)
  - 4 squares 6½" (E)
- 5 strips   3" for outer border

Large floral (violet on ivory)
- 6 strips   5"; from these cut
  - 4 rectangles 5" x 18" (F)
  - 4 rectangles 5" x 23" (G)

Ivory handkerchief linen or quilt-weight cotton
- 4 bias strips 1⅛", total about 2½ yd. long

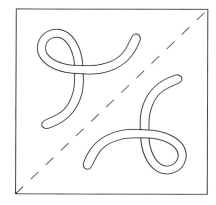

EMBELLISHMENT

Corner Triangles

1. Fold the batiste squares in half diagonally. Finger-press the folds. Trace template 4 (page 95) on all four triangles.

2. Use the lace shaping technique to shape and stitch the insertion lace loops. Fold under the cut ends of the lace about ¼" in a rounded shape.

3. Soak the squares in water to remove the markings and excess starch. Press dry and starch lightly. Trim the fabric from behind the lace.

4. Trim the squares to 12⅛". Cut in half diagonally to form triangles with the lace loop centered in each one.

5. Layer the batiste triangles over the violet triangles; pin and set aside.

Center-Square

1. Fold the 18" batiste square (vertically and horizontally) in quarters and lightly press the creases to use as placement guides. Trace template 5 (page 96) four times around the center.

2. Use the shaped bias strip technique to add bias strips between the lines indicated on the pattern, but do not stitch yet.

3. Use the shaped lace technique to add insertion lace between the indicated lines. Overlap the lace and bias strips to create the interlaced design.

4. Stitch the lace and bias to the base fabric as described in those techniques.

5. Use template 6 (page 97), the 8" linen square, and the turned-edge appliqué (water-soluble stabilizer) technique to prepare the central appliqué motif.

Turning the edges of this motif is the hardest part of the whole quilt, so be patient!

6. Position the appliqué in the center of the interlaced design and stitch in place.

7. Soak the embellished batiste square in water to remove marks, starch, and glue. Press dry and lightly starch.

8. Trim the fabric from behind the lace but not behind the bias strips or appliqué. Trim the square to 16½", carefully centering the interlace design.

9. Layer the batiste square over the violet center square. Pin and set aside.

BORDER

Rickrack and Lace

1. Cut 3" strips of water-soluble stabilizer and piece them together with water-soluble glue to make a strip 58" long. With a blue washout marker and a ruler, draw a straight line about 1" from one long cut edge.

2. Use the rickrack-lace bridging technique to create a rickrack lace strip, with the insertion lace in the center, rickrack on both sides of the center, and lace edging outside the rickrack.

3. Cut the rickrack lace strip into eight 6½" lengths.

Seminole Lacework

1. From the large-floral fabric, cut a strip 2⅜" x 21". From the batiste, cut two strips 2¾" x 21".

2. Using the Seminole lacework technique, make a strip with the large floral as fabric A and the batiste as fabric B. Cut the strip into eight segments 2⅜" and sew them together.

3. Starch and press the sewn strip. Cut it into four equal pieces, by cutting across the widest part of every other floral square.

Wait to add the rickrack lace and Seminole embellishments to B and C until the border strips have been assembled.

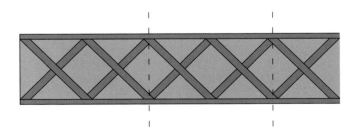

QUILT ASSEMBLY

Center-Square Borders

1. Sew violet accent border strips to the edges of the center square, with butted corners.

2. For the pieced border, use 2 B, 1 C, and 2 D for each border strip, as shown. Press the seam allowances toward the violet pieces. Make four border strips.

3. Add an E square to each end of two of the border strips.

4. Center the Seminole lacework strips over the C rectangles in each border strip. Zigzag (L = 1.0, W = 1.0) near the scalloped edges of the lace edging. Trim the Seminole strips even with raw edges of C.

5. Center the rickrack lace strips over the B rectangles. On the strips without E squares, be sure to allow for the seam allowances when centering the strips. Zigzag as before.

6. Sew the strips without E squares to two opposite sides of the center square. Sew the strips with the E squares to the remaining sides.

7. Sew violet accent strips to the pieced border, with butted corners.

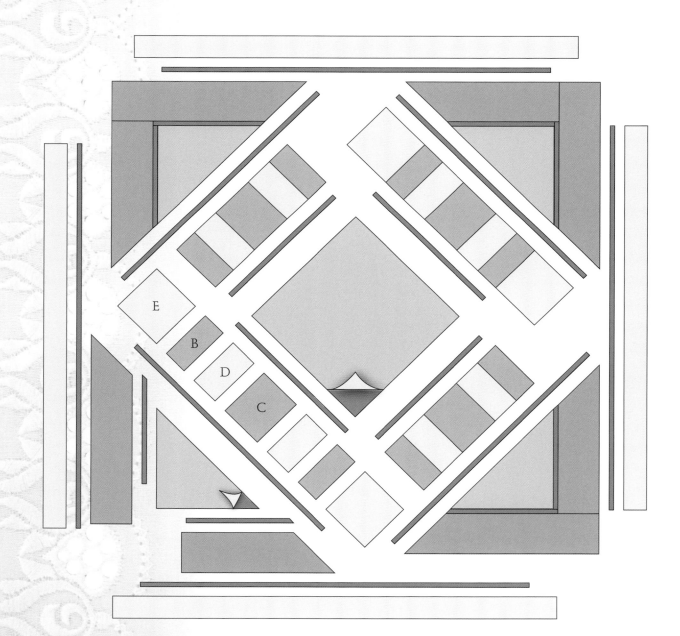

Corner-Triangle Borders

For the corner triangles (A), all the violet border strips and pieces F and G are extra long to allow a margin for error. Align these pieces at the corner of the triangle each time. The other ends of the pieces will extend beyond the bottom of the triangle.

1. From three 1" violet strips, cut four 13" strips and four 14" strips. Sew a 13" strip to one short side of each A triangle. Sew a 14" strip to the other short side of each triangle.

2. Sew a large-floral F to one short side of each triangle then sew a G to other short side.

3. Press these corner triangles carefully to avoid stretching the long bias edges. Square the corners, if necessary, then cut the extra-long strips even with the bottom edge of the triangle .

4. Sew one of these large triangles to each side of the center square.

5. With diagonal seams, join the remaining violet accent strips into one long strip. From it, cut the lengths needed for the remaining borders and sew them to the quilt, with butted corners.

6. Sew the small-floral border strips together into one long strip and sew these to the edges of the quilt as before.

Suggested Quilting

Layer the backing, batting, and quilt top; baste. Use invisible thread to stitch in the ditch along all the seams, lace headings, and bias and appliqué embellishments.

With ivory rayon machine embroidery thread, stipple all the open batiste areas. Outline stitch inside the center appliqué. Stitch a circular loop design in the (E) squares. Channel quilt the outer border.

With violet rayon machine-embroidery thread, free-motion stitch around the outlines of the flowers in the large-floral border.

To finish the raw edges of the quilt, sew the binding strips together, end to end, with diagonal seams. Bind the quilt by using a ½" seam allowance instead of a ¼" allowance, so the binding is the same width as the violet accent strips.

Designed, sewn, and quilted by the author ✎ *36½" x 58"*

Tulips and Twists

TULIPS AND TWISTS

Pin-stitched, appliquéd tulips frame a center panel with twists of shaped puffing and shaped lace. More twists of shaped bias strips embellish the borders.

Techniques
Lace Shaping   page 13
Shaped Bias Strips   page 23
Shaped Puffing   page 26
Turned-Edge Appliqué   page 29

Supplies
Threads
- 60 or 80 wt. ivory cotton
- 50 wt. ivory cotton
- Water-soluble
- Desired Quilting threads

Machine Needles
- 70, 80, and 100 universal

Project Supplies
- ½" bias-tape maker
- ¼" bias-tape maker
- Water-soluble glue or glue stick
- Water-soluble stabilizer
- Blue washout marker
- Freezer paper

Fabrics
Yardages are based on a useable width of at least 41"
- Ivory cotton batiste 3⅜ yd.
- Ivory print 2 yd.
- Peach print ¾ yd.
- Green print 1⅜ yd.
- ⅝" ecru insertion lace 7½ yd.
- 3" wide peach galloon lace (scalloped on both sides) 1 yd.
- Backing 2⅝ yd.
- Batting 44" x 66"

Cutting
Cut strips selvage to selvage, unless lengthwise strips are indicated.

Ivory cotton batiste
- 1 lengthwise strip 13" x 51" (A)
- 2 lengthwise strips 8½" x 51" (B)
- 2 lengthwise strips 6" x 51" (C)
- 6 strips   2¾" for puffing
- 2 strips   6" x 29" (D)
- 4 squares   6" (E)

Green print
- 7 strips   1" x 45" cut lengthwise for sashing
- 5 strips   2¼" x 45" cut lengthwise for binding
- 4 strips   scant ⅝" x 6" for bias stems

Peach Print
- 10 bias strips scant 1⅛" wide (C)

Ivory Print
- 1 strip   12" x 48½" (A)
- 2 strips   7½" x 48½" (B)
- 2 strips   5" x 48½" (C)
- 2 strips   5" x 27" (D)
- 4 squares   5" (E)

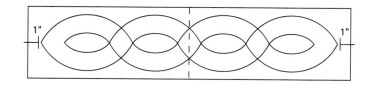

Puffing Panel

1. Fold the batiste A strip in half lengthwise and finger-press the fold.

2. Copy template 7 (page 98) at 200%. Place the template under batiste strip A. (Position the top point of the twist design about 1" from one end of the strip, matching the centerline of the motif with the fabric crease.) Trace the motif.

3. Reposition the template with the points overlapping as shown on the template and trace again. Repeat to make four tracings.

4. Cut the peach galloon lace into four equal pieces. Pin the lace down the center of each twist. Use fine ivory cotton thread and a tiny zigzag (L = 1.5, W = 1.0) to stitch near the scalloped edges of the lace. It is not necessary to stitch across the cut ends.

5. Join the short ends of the batiste puffing strips. Use the shaped puffing technique to gather and shape the strips to the batiste fabric. Then shape and stitch the insertion lace to cover the raw edges of the puffing. Make all the intersections cross in the same direction. Trim the batiste from behind the puffing.

Tulip Appliqué Panels

1. Mark the lengthwise centers of both batiste B strips. Make a mark on the centerline of each strip 8½" from one short end. Make three more marks 11⅛" apart, as in the illustrations.

2. At each mark, trace template 8 (page 99), matching the center mark on the pattern to the marks on the strip. Label one strip "left" and one "right."

3. Use a ¼" bias-tape maker to prepare the green ⅝" x 6" stems. Use water-soluble glue to hold the stems in place, centering them over the traced stem lines. Cut the stems to extend ¼" under the tulips and leaves.

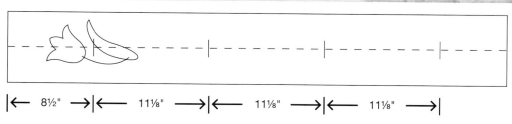

4. Use template 8 and turned-edge appliqué (either water-soluble stabilizer or water-soluble thread) to prepare four left leaves, four right leaves, and eight tulips.

5. Use water-soluble glue or pins to position the appliqués on the batiste strips. Stitch as directed in the technique.

Tulip Corner Squares

1. Find the diagonal centers of the 6" x 6" batiste corner squares (E). Trace template 9 (page 100) onto the squares, centering the design.

2. Prepare the tulip and leaf appliqués in your preferred technique. Glue or pin them in place, placing the raw edges of the leaves under the tulips. Stitch as directed in the technique.

Shaped Bias Panels

1. Fold the batiste C and D strips in half lengthwise and finger-press the creases.

2. Place template 10 (page 101) under a batiste C strip, 1" away from a short end of the strip. Align the template's centerline with the crease. Moving the template as necessary, trace nine twists on the strip.

3. Repeat for the other C strip. In the same manner, trace five twists onto each D strip.

4. At both ends of all four batiste strips, extend the design lines all the way to the edge.

5. Use the shaped bias strip technique to shape and stitch the peach bias strips to the four batiste strips.

Quilt Assembly

1. Soak all embellished batiste pieces in water to remove glue, stabilizer, and markings. Roll in a towel to remove excess water. Air dry and starch the pieces then press on the wrong side.

2. Trim the embellished batiste strips to the same size as their corresponding ivory strips. Layer the batiste strips over the ivory strips, both right side up. Pin together and treat as one.

3. Join the short ends of the 1" green sashing strips to make one long strip. Cutting lengths from the long strip as needed, sew sashing on both long edges of both tulip panels.

4. Sew the tulip panels to the puffing panel, making sure the tulips curve toward the puffing. Add the C panels to the sides of the quilt.

5. Sew sashing strips to the top and bottom of the quilt then sew sashing strips to both short ends of the D panels.

6. Sew E squares to both D panels. (Position the E squares so the tulips point toward the corners of the quilt.) Sew the D-E strips to the top and bottom of the quilt.

7. Stay-stitch around the edges of the quilt top ⅛" from the raw edges to hold the layers together.

Suggested Quilting

Layer the backing, batting, and quilt top; baste. Use invisible thread to quilt in the ditch of all sashing seams, appliqué motifs, and bias strips. Quilt along both edges of all lace strips.

With iridescent peach and green threads, quilt free-form vein details in the leaves and petal details in the tulips. Quilt along the design elements in the lace inside the puffing.

With variegated ivory-tan thread, quilt free-form feathers outside the puffing. Quilt swirls outside the tulips, feathers inside the shaped bias twists, and stippling outside the twists.

Add binding to finish the raw edges of the quilt.

Designed and sewn by the author, quilted by Lin Hayden ✣ *90" x 90"*

Springtime Heirloom

SPRINGTIME HEIRLOOM

Blocks of white batiste embellished with insertion lace or bias linen Celtic loops are layered over a yellow tone-on-tone print. Large-and small-scale yellow, green, and rose florals and a green fabric form the borders and sashing. Narrow borders and a binding of deep rose add a bright accent. Decorative stitching and digitized machine embroidery accent the blocks.

Techniques
Lace Shaping   page 13
Shaped Bias Strips   page 23

Supplies
Threads
- Machine embroidery thread, to coordinate with fabrics
- Sewing thread to blend with fabrics
- Fine white cotton
- Desired quilting threads

Machine Needles
- 80 universal
- 100 or 110 universal for pin stitch

Project Supplies
- ½" bias-tape maker
- Water-soluble glue (optional)
- Washout marker
- Digitized machine embroidery (optional)
- Zundt200250rosebud
- Zundt202016lacebow
  (free downloads from www.zundtdesign.com)
- Tearaway stabilizer
- Heavyweight water-soluble stabilizer

Fabrics
Yardages are based on a useable width of at least 40"
- White cotton batiste 3¾ yd.
- Yellow 3½ yd.
- Green 2 yd.
- Small floral (yellow, green, rose) 2½ yd.
- Large floral (yellow, green, rose) 2¾ yd.
- Rose 1¼ yd.
- White handkerchief linen 1¼ yd.
- ⅝" wide white insertion lace 30 yd.
- Backing 8⅝ yd.
- Batting 98" x 98"

Cutting
Cut strips selvage to selvage, unless lengthwise strips are indicated
White cotton batiste
- 25 squares 13½" for blocks
Yellow
- 25 squares 12½" for block backgrounds
Small floral
- 6 strips   2¼"; from these cut
  - 100 squares 2¼" (A)
- 25 strips   1½" for sashing (C) and borders
- 10 strips   3"; from these cut
  - 60 rectangles 3" x 2¼" (D)
  - 24 rectangles 3" x 6½" (E)
  - 12 rectangles 3" x 4¾" (F)
Green
- 49 strips 1¼" for sashing (B) and borders
Large Floral
- 4 lengthwise strips 5" x 92½" for borders
Rose
- 19 strips ¾" for borders
- 10 strips 2¼" for binding
White handkerchief linen
- 1⅛" wide bias strips for Celtic loops, as needed

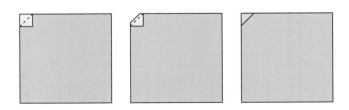

Block Embellishments

1. Starch well and press the batiste squares. Fold each square, vertically and horizontally, into quarters. Finger-press the folds. Trace template 11 (page 102) on each square with a washout marker.

2. For the Celtic loops, use the shaped bias strips technique to stitch bias linen strips on 13 batiste squares, placing the outer edge of the strips along the traced lines. Overlap the loops as shown in the photo.

3. Use the lace shaping technique to stitch the lace on 12 batiste squares, placing the outer edge along the traced lines. Overlap the loops as with the bias strips.

4. Soak the blocks in water to remove the markings and water-soluble glue, if used. Roll the squares in a towel to remove excess water. Air dry. Starch and press.

For the quilt in the photo on page 61, the batiste squares were lightly tea-dyed after soaking, because the soft white looked better than pure white with the background fabrics.

5. With the loop designs centered, trim the blocks to 12½" x 12½".

6. If using digitized machine embroidery, stitch a rosebud or other small floral motif in the center of all the squares. (Use a tearaway stabilizer under the fabrics.)

Notice that the embroidery designs in the lace blocks mirror those in the bias strip blocks.

7. Select one of the thread colors in the machine embroidery and sew a tiny machine feather stitch (L = 2.0, W = 2.0) or other decorative stitch ¼" outside the Celtic loop design. Use a stabilizer, if necessary, to prevent puckering.

8. Layer each batiste square over a yellow square. Pin them together and treat as one layer from here on.

9. With right sides together, place an A square on each corner of every block. Sew diagonally from corner to corner. Trim the seam allowances to ¼". Open the triangles and press.

QUILT ASSEMBLY
Sashing

1. Sew a green B strip to both sides of 15 small-floral C strips. Press. Cut the strips into 60 pieces 9" long.

2. Sew small-floral D rectangles to both ends of 30 of the pieces to complete the vertical sashing strips. Press.

3. Sew the remaining 30 pieces together in six groups of five, with small-floral E rectangles in between.

4. Sew a small-floral F to both ends of each strip to complete the horizontal sashing rows.

5. Sew the blocks and vertical sashing into horizontal rows, alternating the pieces as shown in the quilt assembly diagram.

6. Sew the block rows and horizontal sashing rows together, starting and ending with a sashing row.

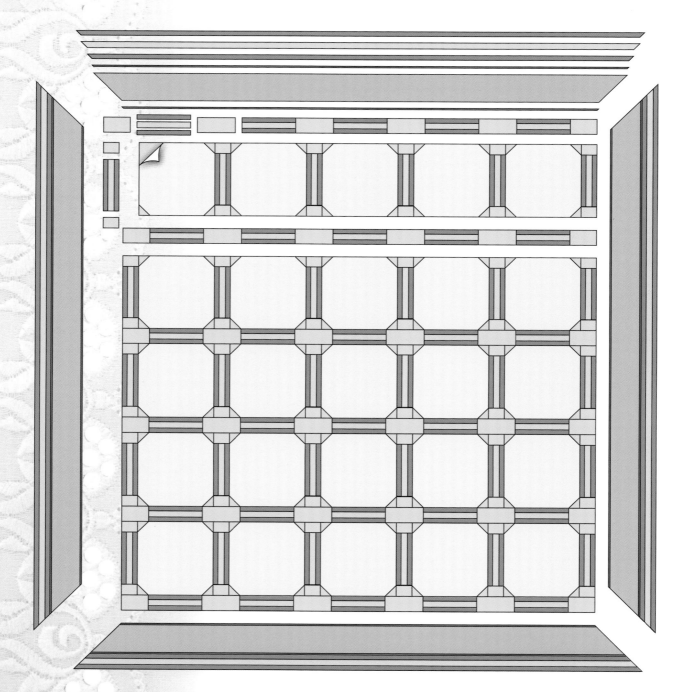

Borders

The border strips are extra long to allow for custom fitting. Trim off the extra length after sewing them to the quilt.

1. Sew the small-floral border strips, end to end with diagonal seams, to make one long strip. Press. Repeat for the remaining green strips and then the rose strips.

2. Cut the long strips into 92½" lengths as needed. Referring to the quilt photo and assembly diagram for color arrangement, sew the strips into four border units.

3. Pin and sew all four border units to the quilt top and miter the corners.

Suggested Quilting

Layer the backing, batting, and quilt top; baste. The quilt shown was longarm quilted with in-the-ditch and echo quilting in the blocks, free-form feathers in the borders, and eight-petaled flowers in the octagon-shaped small floral cornerstones.

If using digitized machine embroidery, stitch 36 freestanding lace bows from Zundt202016lacebow or other small, freestanding lace motif on heavy water-soluble stabilizer. Soak the embroideries well to dissolve the stabilizer. Air-dry then press the embroideries. Stitch the lace bows to the center of the octagon-shaped, small-floral cornerstones, through all the layers, by stitching a small circle around the "knot" of the bow only, leaving the rest of the bow free.

Add binding to finish the raw edges of the quilt.

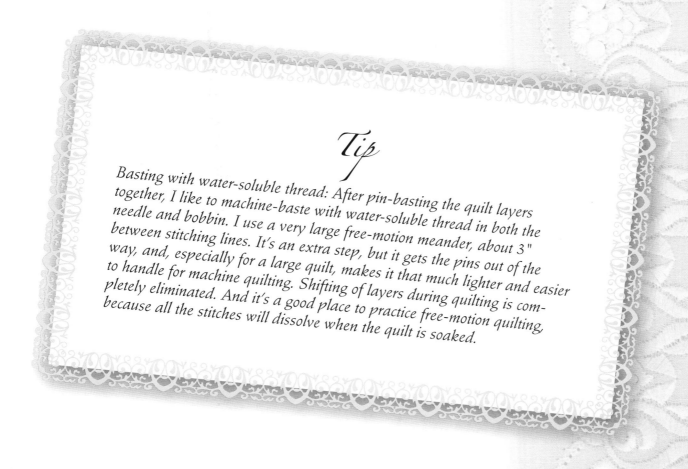

Tip

Basting with water-soluble thread: After pin-basting the quilt layers together, I like to machine-baste with water-soluble thread in both the needle and bobbin. I use a very large free-motion meander, about 3" between stitching lines. It's an extra step, but it gets the pins out of the way, and, especially for a large quilt, makes it that much lighter and easier to handle for machine quilting. Shifting of layers during quilting is completely eliminated. And it's a good place to practice free-motion quilting, because all the stitches will dissolve when the quilt is soaked.

Designed, sewn, and quilted by the author ❧ *54" x 67½"*

Just Peachy

JUST PEACHY

This sampler quilt features almost every technique, from lace shaping through transparent reverse-appliqué windows. Decorative machine stitching adds beautiful accents. The sashing and borders are made with a border print, and wide peach lace outlines the quilt.

❦ Techniques

❦ Supplies

Threads
- Machine embroidery, to coordinate with fabrics
- Sewing thread to blend with fabrics
- Fine white cotton
- Desired quilting threads

Machine Needles
- 70 universal
- 80 universal
- 100 or 110 universal
- 100 wing
- 1.6/80 or 2.0/80 twin

Project Supplies
- ½" bias-tape maker
- 5- or 7- groove pintuck foot (optional)
- Heavy water-soluble stabilizer
- Lightweight tear-away stabilizer
- Blue washout marker
- Water-soluble glue (optional)

Fabrics
Yardages are based on a useable width of at least 40"
- White cotton batiste 3⅛ yd.
- Tone-on-tone peach 2⅞ yd.
- Small-floral peach 1 yd.
- Small-floral lengthwise stripe 1½ yd.
  (Yardage assumes cutting 7 like stripes 2¼" to 2½" wide.)
- Large-floral lengthwise stripe 1½ yd.

- White handkerchief linen ¼ yd.
- English cotton netting or tulle (preshrunk) 11" x 11"
- White pre-tucked lightweight cotton *(or sew three ⅛" tucks in batiste)* ⅛ yd.
- White silk organza or cotton organdy 10" x 10"
- 2½" wide white cotton embroidered eyelet insertion ⅓ yd.
- ¼" wide white cotton rickrack ⅔ yd.
- ⅝" wide white insertion lace 4¼ yd.
- 1" wide white insertion lace ⅔ yd.
- ¾" wide white edging lace 4 yd.
- 3"–3¼" wide peach edging lace 7⅜ yd.
- Backing 2¼ yd. (60" wide)
- Batting 62" x 75"

❦ Cutting

Cut strips selvage to selvage, unless lengthwise strips are indicated.

White cotton batiste
- 2 lengthwise strips 3¾" x 70" for side borders
- 2 lengthwise strips 3¾" x 56½" for top and bottom borders
- 9 squares 14" for blocks
- 1 strip 2½" x 40" for puffing
- 1 rectangle 10" x 12" for pintucks
- 2 bias rectangles 3" x 10" for lace windows
- 2 rectangles 4" x 10" for lace windows

Tone-on-tone peach
- 2 lengthwise strips 3¾" x 70" for side borders
- 2 lengthwise strips 3¾" x 56½" for top and bottom borders
- 9 squares 13" for block backgrounds

Small-floral peach
- 3 strips 2¼"; from these cut
  - 36 squares 2¼" x 2¼" (A)
- 4 strips 3"; from these cut
  - 24 rectangles 3" x 2¼" (C)
  - 8 rectangles 3" x 4¾" (D)
  - 8 rectangles 3" x 6½" (E)
- 7 strips 2¼" for binding

Small-floral stripe
- 7 lengthwise strips 3" with stripes centered; from these cut
  - 2 strips 3" x 49½" for borders
  - 24 rectangles 3" x 9½" (B)

Large-floral stripe
- 2 lengthwise strips 4¾" x 49½" for top and bottom borders

REVERSE APPLIQUÉ WINDOWS

Block Embellishment

Use lightweight tearaway stabilizer under the fabric for all decorative machine stitching.

1. Fold a 14" batiste square into quarters diagonally. Finger-press the folds. Trace template 12 (page 103) onto the square with a washout marker.

2. Use the reverse appliqué windows technique with a 10" square of silk organza or cotton organdy for the reverse appliqué.

3. Sew a tiny decorative machine stitch along the lines indicated in the pattern.

RICKRACK LACE BRIDGING

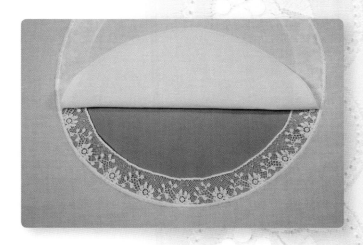

1. Fold a 14" batiste square, vertically and horizontally, into quarters. Finger-press the folds. Trace the outer circle from template 13 (page 104) onto the square with a washout marker.

2. Use the lace shaping technique to place ¾" lace edging inside the drawn circle, with the scalloped edge along the marked line. Sew the scalloped edge *only*, zigzagging just inside the edge instead of over it, as for a header.

3. On the wrong side, trim away the fabric behind the lace close to stitching. You are cutting a large, lace-trimmed hole in your block.

4. Cut one 10" length of 1" wide insertion lace (a), two 10" lengths of ⅝" wide insertion lace (b), and two 10" lengths of baby rickrack (c). Use the rickrack-lace bridging technique to make a strip in the order b/c/a/c/b.

5. Place the rickrack-lace strip over the circle of fabric cut from behind the lace. Use the joining lace to fabric (three-step method) described on page 13 to sew the outer edges of the strip to the circle.

6. Sew a tiny decorative machine stitch ⅜" from the outer edges of the rickrack-lace strip.

7. Place the lace-embellished circle back under the lace-trimmed hole in the block, aligning the rickrack-lace strip vertically. Zigzag (L = 0.5–0.7, W = 2.5) over the inner header of the lace circle. Trim the fabric from behind the lace circle.

8. Sew a tiny decorative machine stitch ⅜" outside the outer edge of the lace edging.

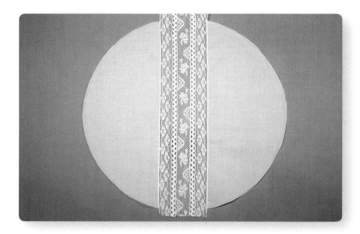

SHAPED LACE WITH PINTUCKS

1. Fold a 14" batiste square, vertically and horizontally, into quarters. Finger-press the folds. Trace template 14 (page 105) onto the square with a washout marker.

2. Use the lace shaping technique to shape ⅝" insertion lace inside the drawn lines. Sew along the outer header of the lace *only*.

3. On the wrong side, trim away the fabric behind the lace close to stitching, creating a large, lace-trimmed hole in the block.

4. Using the twin-needle pintuck technique, steps 1–4, sew pintucks along the 10" length of the 10" x 12" batiste rectangle. Sew a wide enough section of pintucks to fill the lace-trimmed hole in the block.

5. Place the pintucked fabric under the lace-trimmed block, aligning the tucks vertically. Zigzag (L = 0.5–0.7, W = 2.5) over the inner lace header. Trim the fabric from behind the lace.

6. Using the shaped pintuck technique, sew a pintuck ¼" outside the lace, pivoting on the marked lines. Sew a second pintuck outside the first, using the edge of the foot as a guide.

7. Sew a tiny decorative machine stitch along the line indicated in the pattern.

NETTING INSERTION

1. Fold a 14" batiste square, vertically and horizontally, into quarters. Finger-press the folds. Trace template 15 (page 106) onto the square with a washout marker.

2. Use the 11" x 11" square of preshrunk netting or tulle and follow the netting insertions technique to embellish the batiste square.

3. Sew decorative machine scallops, in a color to match the netting, around the outer edge of the lace circle so that the scallops point toward the center of the circle and the points of the scallops just touch the entredeux or satin stitching.

4. Sew a tiny decorative machine stitch just outside the outer edge of the scallops and ¼" inside the central diamond shape.

SEMINOLE LACEWORK

1. Follow steps 1–3 for the rickrack-lace bridging block (page 69).

2. Using the Seminole lacework technique make a strip with the following pieces: cotton embroidered eyelet insertion, trimmed to 2⅜" wide (fabric A); pre-tucked batiste 2¾" wide (fabric B); and ⅝" wide insertion lace. Cut the strips 10" long and cut four 2⅜" segments from the strips.

3. Place the Seminole lacework strip over the circle of fabric cut from behind the lace, centering the circle under the strip. Use the joining lace to

fabric (three-step method) described on page 13 to sew the outer edges of the strip to the circle. Sew a tiny decorative machine stitch ⅜" from the outer edges of the lacework strip.

4. Place the embellished circle back under the lace-trimmed hole in the block, aligning the Seminole strip vertically. Zigzag (L = 0.5–0.7, W = 2.5) over the inner header of the lace circle. Trim the fabric from behind the lace circle.

5. Sew a tiny decorative machine stitch ⅜" outside the outer edge of the lace edging.

SHAPED PUFFING

1. Fold a 14" batiste square, vertically and horizontally, into quarters. Finger-press the folds. Trace template 13 (page 104) onto the square with a washout marker.

2. Use the shaped puffing technique to embellish this block. For the puffing, use the 2½" x 40" strip of batiste. Pull up the gathers so the strip measures about 28" long. Cut off the end of the puffing strip 1" beyond the starting point. Turn under ½" on this end, overlapping the raw edge by ½".

3. Shape ⅝" insertion lace on the inside edge of the puffing and ¾" lace edging on the outer edge of the puffing, with the scalloped edge along the marked line. After trimming the base fabric behind the puffing and lace, zigzag over the turned-under ends of the puffing lace right along the fold lines.

4. Sew a tiny decorative machine stitch ⅜" outside the outer edge of the lace edging and ⅜" inside the inner lace circle.

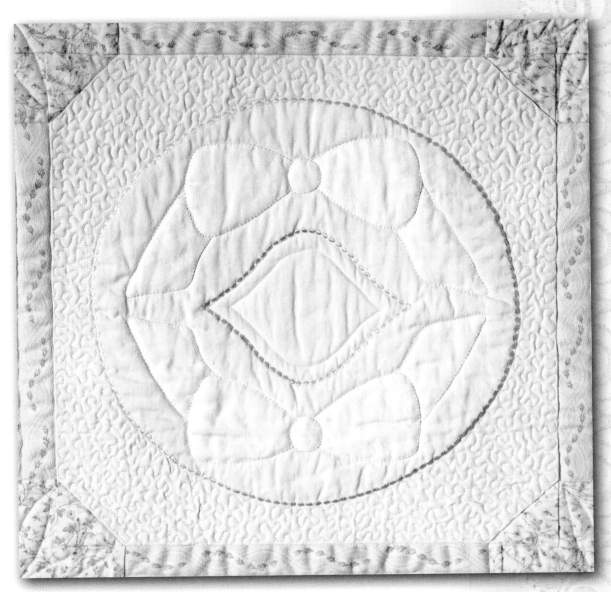

APPLIQUÉ BOW

1. Fold a 14" batiste square, vertically and horizontally, into quarters. Finger-press the folds. Trace template 16 (page 107) onto the square with a washout marker.

2. Use turned-edge appliqué, with either the water-soluble facing or the water-soluble thread technique, to prepare and sew linen bows to the batiste square. The dashed lines on the appliqué templates indicate raw edges.

3. Sew a tiny decorative machine stitch along the lines indicated in the pattern. Use a stabilizer to prevent puckering.

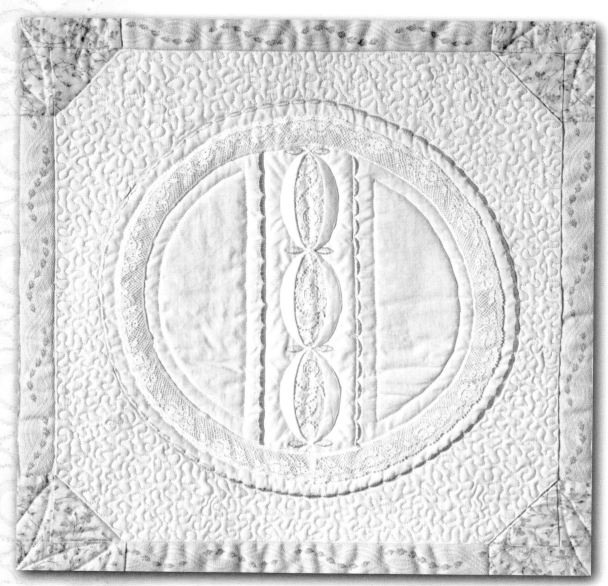

CATHEDRAL LACE WINDOWS

1. Follow steps 1–3 from the rickrack-lace bridging block (page 69).

2. Using the cathedral lace windows technique, make a strip with the following dimensions: two 3" x 10" batiste bias strips and 1" wide insertion lace. Place four bar tacks 2½" apart, centered along the length of the strip. Trim the strip to an even 2¾" width, measuring out 1⅜" on each side of the center.

3. Sew the 10" sides of the 4" x 10" batiste rectangles to the long raw edges of the cathedral lace strip, right sides together. Press the seam allowances away from the strip. Stitch over the seam and seam allowances from the right side with a decorative machine stitch.

4. If desired, machine sew a little satin-stitch oval or heart on both sides of each bar tack, between the lace windows.

5. Place the lace strip under the lace-trimmed hole in the block, aligning the strip vertically. Zigzag (L = 0.5–0.7, W = 2.5) over the inner header of the lace circle. Trim the fabric from behind the lace circle.

6. Sew a tiny decorative machine stitch ⅜" outside the outer edge of the lace edging.

SHAPED CELTIC LOOPS

1. Fold a 14" batiste square, vertically and horizontally, into quarters. Finger-press the folds. Trace template 11 (page 102) onto the square with a washout marker.

2. Use the shaped bias strips technique to shape and sew the bias linen strips, placing the outer edges of the strips along the traced lines.

3. Sew a tiny decorative machine stitch ¼" outside the outer edges of the Celtic loop design and ¼" inside the central diamond shape.

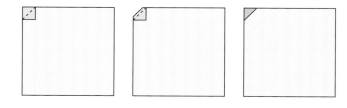

Quilt Assembly

Blocks and sashing

1. Soak all the embellished batiste blocks in water to remove marks, water-soluble stabilizer, and water-soluble glue, if used. Air dry. Lightly starch and press.

2. With the designs centered, trim the blocks to 13" x 13".

3. Layer the batiste blocks over the tone-on-tone peach squares. Pin the squares together and treat them as one piece from here on.

4. With right sides together, place an A square on each corner of every block, as shown in the figure. Sew diagonally from corner to corner. Trim the seam allowances to ¼". Open the triangles and press.

5. To make the sashing strips, sew C rectangles to both short ends of 12 B rectangles. Press open.

6. Sew three blocks and four sashing strips together to make a block row. Make three block rows, as shown in the quilt assembly diagram.

7. Referring to the quilt assembly diagram, join 3 B, 2 D, and 2 E, end to end, to make a sashing row. Make four sashing rows.

8. Sew the block rows and sashing rows together, starting and ending with a sashing row.

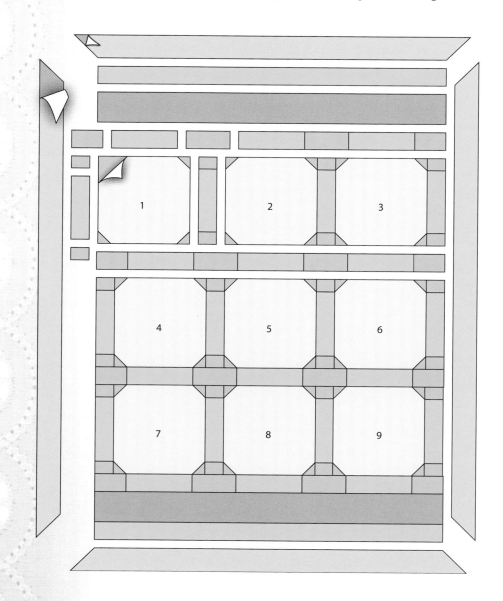

Borders

Border strips are extra long to allow for custom fitting. Trim off the extra length after sewing them to the quilt.

1. Sew the large-floral border strips to the top and bottom of quilt top. Press.

2. Sew small-floral border strips to the top and bottom of the quilt top. Press.

3. To prepare the border strips, layer a 3¾" x 56½" batiste strip over a 3¾" x 56½" peach strip. Pin the fabrics together and treat as one. Repeat for the other 56½" batiste and peach strips and for the 3¾" x 70" batiste and peach strips.

4. Place the straight edge of the 3"–3¼" wide peach lace edging about ⅛" in from one long, raw edge of each border strip. Straight-stitch the lace headers, close to the edge, through all the layers. Sew a tiny zigzag (L = 1.5, W = 1.0) with fine thread near the scalloped edge of the lace through all the layers.

5. With the plain edge of the border strip next to the raw edge of the quilt top, pin and sew the borders to the quilt and miter the corners.

Suggested Quilting

Layer the backing, batting, and quilt top; baste. With invisible thread, stitch in the ditch along all the lace and fabric seams. Stitch along any stripes in the striped sashing. Quilt along any decorative stitching and along alternate pintucks.

With peach machine embroidery thread, meander stitch in the open batiste areas of the blocks and outline stitch inside the larger plain areas inside the embellished circles. Quilt eight-petal flowers in the octagon-shaped, small-floral cornerstones.

Free-motion stitch, following prominent lines in both the large-floral stripe borders and within the wide peach lace border.

Add binding to finish the raw edges of the quilt.

Designed, sewn, and quilted by the author ✤ 17" x 17"

Blue Heirloom Pillows

Blue Heirloom Pillows

Any of the blocks fom the Just Peachy sampler quilt can be made into a pillow. Three of the blocks are shown here.

Techniques

Joining Lace to Fabric	page 12
Lace Shaping	page 13
Cathedral Lace Windows	page 21
Seminole Lacework	page 23
Shaped Puffing	page 26

Supplies

Threads

- Sewing thread to blend with fabric
- Medium-blue machine embroidery
- White machine embroidery
- Fine white cotton
- Desired quilting threads

Project Supplies

- 2 buttons
- 16" pillow form
- Blue washout marker
- Lightweight tearaway stabilizer

Fabrics for EACH Pillow

Yardages are based on a useable width of at least 40"

- Light Blue fabric ⅔ yd.
- Medium blue fabric ⅔ yd.
- Muslin or backing fabric 21" x 21"
- Batting 21" x 21"

Additional Requirements

Shaped puffing pillow

- White cotton batiste
  1 square 13½"
  1 strip 2½" x 40"
- ⅝" wide white insertion lace 1½ yd.
- Water-soluble glue (optional)

Cathedral lace window pillow

- White cotton batiste
  1 square 13½"
  2 bias strips 3" x 10"
  2 rectangles 4" x 10"
- ⅝" wide white insertion lace 1 yd.
- 1" wide white insertion lace ⅓ yd.
- Water-soluble glue (optional)

Seminole Lacework pillow

- White cotton batiste
  1 square 13½"
- 2½" wide white cotton embroidered eyelet insertion ⅓ yd.
- Two strips 2¾" x 10" pre-tucked white fabric (or use batiste and stitch three ⅛" tucks)
- ⅝" wide white insertion lace 3½ yd.

Cutting Per Block

Cut strips selvage to selvage.

Medium Blue

- 1 square 12½"
- 2 strips 1¼" (A)
- 2 strips 2½" for binding

Light Blue

- 1 strip 11⅝"; from this cut
  - 2 rectangles 11⅝" x 17" for pillow back
  - 4 squares 2¼" (B)
- 1 strip 1½" (C)
- 1 strip 3"; from this cut
  - 4 rectangles 2¼" x 3" (D)
  - 4 rectangles 3" x 4¾" (E)

Shaped Puffing Pillow

1. Trace template 13 (page 104) on the batiste square with a blue washout marker.

2. Use the shaped puffing technique to shape and stitch a 2½" x 40" strip of batiste. Pull up the gathers until the strip measures about 28". Cut off the end of the puffing strip 1" beyond the starting point and turn under ½" of the end, overlapping the raw edge by ½".

3. Use the lace shaping technique to add insertion lace along the inner and outer edges of the puffing.

4. After trimming fabric from behind the lace, zigzag over all the turned-under ends of the lace and puffing, right along the fold line.

5. With white machine embroidery thread and stabilizer under the fabric, stitch a decorative scallop around the outer edge of the large lace circle, so that the points of the scallops just touch the outer edge of the lace.

6. With blue machine embroidery thread and stabilizer, stitch small decorative stitches (satin stitch ovals were used in sample) ¼" outside scallops, and ¼" inside the inner edge of the small lace circle.

Cathedral Lace Window Pillow

1. Trace the outer circle from template 13 (page 104) on the batiste square with a blue washout marker.

2. Use the lace shaping technique to add insertion lace inside the drawn circle, with the outer edge of the lace along the marked line. Stitch along the outer edge of the lace only.

3. On the wrong side, trim away the fabric behind the lace close to the stitching. You are cutting a large, lace-trimmed hole in your block.

4. Using the two 3" x 10" bias strips of batiste and 1" wide insertion lace, follow the technique for cathedral lace windows, placing four bar tacks 2½" apart. Trim the strip to an even 2¾" width, measuring out 1⅜" on each side of the center.

5. Sew the 10" sides of the 4" x 10" batiste rectangles to the long raw edges of the window strip, right sides together. Press the seam allowances away from the strip.

6. Stitch over the seams and seam allowances, from the right side, with a decorative machine stitch, using tearaway stabilizer under the fabric.

7. If desired, machine stitch a little satin-stitch oval on both sides of the bar tacks, between the lace windows (Use a stabilizer under the fabric.)

8. Place the lace window square under the lace-trimmed hole in the block, lining up the lace window strip vertically. Zigzag (L = 0.5 – 0.7, W = 2.5) over the inner header of the lace circle. Trim the fabric from behind the lace.

9. With white machine embroidery thread and stabilizer, stitch a decorative scallop around the outer edge of the lace circle, so that the points of the scallops just touch the outer edge of the lace.

10. With blue machine embroidery thread and stabilizer, stitch a small decorative stitch (satin stitch ovals were used in the sample) ¼" outside the scallops.

Seminole Lacework Pillow

1. Follow steps 1 and 2 for the Cathedral Lace Window Pillow (page 83).

2. Use the Seminole lacework technique to make a Seminole lacework strip. Use cotton embroidered eyelet insertion, trimmed to 2⅜" wide, for fabric A and pre-tucked batiste for fabric B. Cut strips 10" long, and cut four 2⅜" segments from the strips.

3. Place the Seminole lacework strip over the circle of fabric cut from behind the lace, centering the circle under the strip. Use the joining lace to fabric (three-step method) to stitch the outer edges of the strip.

4. With white machine embroidery thread and stabilizer, stitch a decorative scallop along the edge of the lace border strips, so that the points of the scallops just touch the outer edge of the lace.

5. Place the embellished circle back under the lace-trimmed hole in the block, lining up the Seminole strip vertically. Zigzag (L = 0.5–0.7, W = 2.5) over the inner header of the lace circle. Trim fabric from behind the lace.

6. With white machine embroidery thread and stabilizer, stitch a decorative scallop around the outer edge of the lace circle, so that the points of the scallops just touch the outer edge of the lace.

7. With blue machine embroidery thread and stabilizer, stitch a small decorative stitch (satin stitch ovals were used in the sample) ¼" outside the scallops.

Completing the Pillow Top

1. Soak the embellished batiste square in water to remove marks and water-soluble glue, if used.

2. Trim the square to 12½" x 12½", with the design centered.

3. Layer the batiste square over the 12½" x 12½" medium blue square. Pin together and treat as one block from here on.

4. With right sides together, place a light blue B square on each corner of the block, aligning the raw edges. Sew the square diagonally from corner to corner. Trim the seam allowances to ¼". Open the triangles and press.

5. Sew a medium blue A strip to both long edges of a light blue C strip. Press and cut into four 9" lengths.

6. To two of the A-C strips, sew the light blue D rectangles to both ends. Sew these strips to opposite sides of the block.

7. To the two remaining border A-C strips, sew the light blue E rectangles to both ends. Sew these strips to the remaining sides of the block.

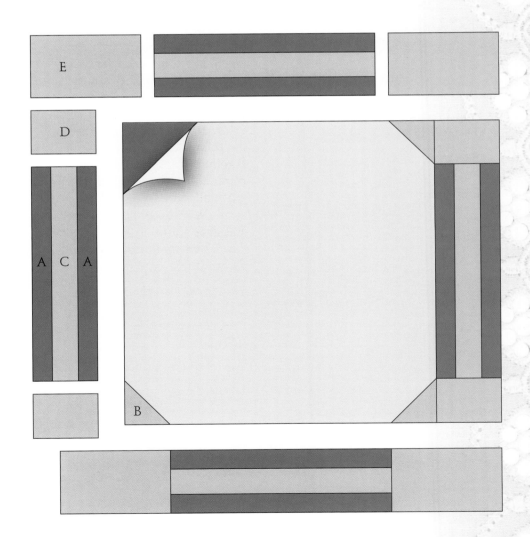

Suggested Quilting

Layer the backing, batting, and pillow top; baste. With invisible thread, stitch in the ditch of all fabric and lace seams, and along the decorative stitching.

With blue machine embroidery thread, quilt freeform swirled feathers in the light blue corners.

With white machine embroidery thread, quilt freeform feathers in the open spaces in the circles and meander stitching in the batiste area outside the circles.

Completing the Pillow

1. Stay-stitch ⅛" from the outer edge of the pillow top. Trim away excess batting and backing then square the corners.

2. On one long edge of both light blue 11⅝" x 17" rectangles, press under 1¼", then 1¼" again. On one rectangle, mark 2½" on each side of the center on the placket. Stitch buttonholes at the marks.

3. Lay the rectangles right side up, with the plackets overlapping and the buttonhole piece on top. Mark the placement for the buttons on the plain back piece. Sew buttons at the marks.

4. Button the pillow-back pieces together. Trim the pillow back to the same size as the pillow top. Pin the ends of the plackets together.

5. Place the quilted top and the buttoned back wrong sides together. Baste around the edges.

6. Sew the binding strips together with diagonal seams. Apply the binding to the pillow.

7. Unbutton the pillow back and insert the pillow form.

Heirloom Baby Bonnets, designed and sewn by the author

Heirloom Baby Bonnets

PALE PINK BONNET

These sweet little bonnets are quick to make; require only a little fabric, lace, and ribbon; and provide a great way to practice techniques on a small project. Even if you don't have a baby in your life, they make wonderful gifts. The widths of the laces can be changed to use up bits and pieces remaining from other projects or to incorporate lace from an old handkerchief or baby gown. The bonnets can be made smaller or larger, and the ribbon casing in back allows for adjustment in size and laying flat for pressing.

 ### Fabric and Supplies
- Pale pink batiste rectangle 7" x 13"
- ½" wide pale pink edging lace 13"
- 1½" wide pale pink insertion lace 13"
- ⅝" wide pale pink silk satin ribbon 1 yd.
- ⅛" wide pale pink silk satin ribbon ⅝ yd.
- Machine embroidery thread to match fabric and lace
- Fine cotton thread to match lace
- Water-soluble stabilizer
- Washout marker

Bonnet Assembly

1. Starch and press the batiste rectangle. With a washout marker, draw a line 1¼" from one long edge of the rectangle.

2. Place stabilizer under the rectangle. Use machine embroidery thread to sew a row of decorative stitching along the drawn line.

You may need to reduce the size of the preset stitch to get a smaller design, more in scale for a baby.

3. Select a different stitch and sew a row on both sides of the first stitching. The three rows should make a pattern about ¾" wide.

I like to use water-soluble stabilizer instead of tear-away so that no scratchy bits of stabilizer are left in the stitching.

4. Soak the batiste in water to completely remove the stabilizer. Starch and press.

5. Draw lines ¼" outside both sides of the decorative stitching. Place the straight edge of the lace edging on the line closest to the raw edge. Place the edge of the insertion along the other line. Use the joining lace to fabric technique (three-step method, page 13) to stitch the lace.

6. Measuring from the scalloped edge of the lace edging, trim the batiste rectangle to 6½" x 12".

7. To hem the 6½" edge, press under ¼", then ¼" again. Stitch the hem. Repeat for the other 6½" edge.

8. On the long raw edge of the batiste, press under ⅛" then ⅜". Stitch close to first pressed edge to form the ribbon casing. Backstitch at both ends to secure the stitching. Using a bodkin or small safety pin, run the ⅛" ribbon through casing.

9. Cut the ⅝" wide ribbon in half for the ties. Use a bit of sealant to prevent the cut ends from fraying.

10. On one end of each ribbon tie, fold under 1" (do not press). About ¾" from the fold, take a tiny tuck, so the loop looks like half a bow.

11. Referring to the photo, pin a ribbon to the edge of the bonnet, about 1" in from the scalloped edge of the lace. Stitch securely across the tuck and through the narrow hem of the bonnet to hold the ribbon in place. Repeat for the other side of the bonnet.

12. Pull up the narrow ribbon in the casing until the fabric is in snug gathers. Tie the narrow ribbon in a bow.

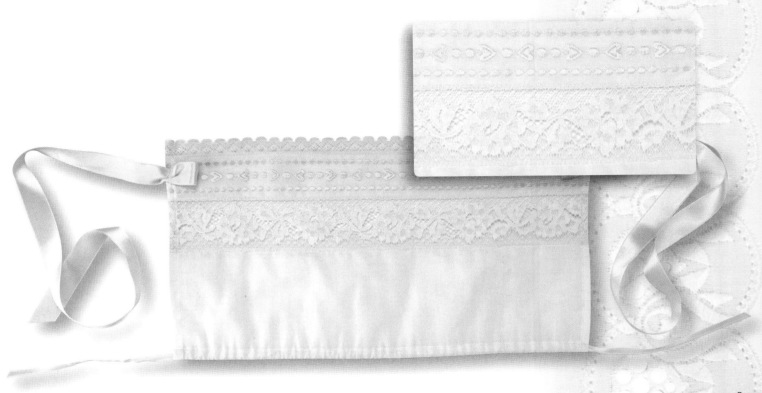

PALE BLUE PINTUCKED BONNET

☺ Fabric and Supplies

- Pale blue batiste rectangle 8" x 13"
- ¾" wide ivory edging lace 13"
- ⅝" wide ivory insertion lace, 3 strips 13"
- ⅝" wide pale blue silk satin ribbon 1 yd.
- ⅛" wide pale blue silk satin ribbon ⅝ yd.
- Blue washout marker

Threads

- Fine ivory cotton
- Fine pale blue cotton
- Pale blue #12 pearl cotton (optional)

Machine Needle

- 1.6/80 or 2.0/80 twin needle
- 5-groove or 7-groove pintuck foot

Bonnet Assembly

1. With the washout marker, draw a line 1¾" from one long edge of the batiste rectangle.

2. Use the twin-needle pintuck technique (page 18) to stitch a pintuck on the drawn line.

Cording was used on the bonnet shown, but this is optional.

3. Stitch two more pintucks on both sides of the first one. Starch and press the fabric on the wrong side.

4. Stitch the three 13" strips of ivory insertion lace together, using the joining lace to lace technique (page 12).

5. With a washout marker, draw a line ¼" outside both outermost pintucks.

6. Place the straight edge of the edging lace on the line closest to the raw edge of the batiste. Place the edge of the insertion lace along the other line. Stitch the laces in place using the joining lace to fabric technique (three-step method, page 13).

7. Complete the bonnet by using steps 6 through 12 for the pale pink bonnet (page 89).

WHITE LACE AND RICKRACK BONNET

✿ Fabric and Supplies

- White batiste rectangle 4½" x 13"
- 1¼" wide white edging lace 13"
- ½" wide white insertion lace, 3 strips 13"
- ¼" wide white cotton rickrack 1¼ yd.
- ⅝" wide white silk satin ribbon 1 yd.
- ⅛" wide white silk satin ribbon ⅝ yd.
- Water-soluble stabilizer
- Water-soluble glue
- Fine white cotton thread

Bonnet Assembly

1. Use the rickrack-lace bridging technique (page 20) to prepare a rickrack and lace edging piece with the strips in the order shown in the figure.

2. Soak the strip to remove all traces of the stabilizer. Starch and press.

3. Place the insertion edge of the lace ½" over one long raw edge of the batiste rectangle. Stitch by using the joining lace to fabric technique (three-step method).

4. Complete the bonnet using steps 6 through 12 for the pale pink bonnet (page 89).

Templates

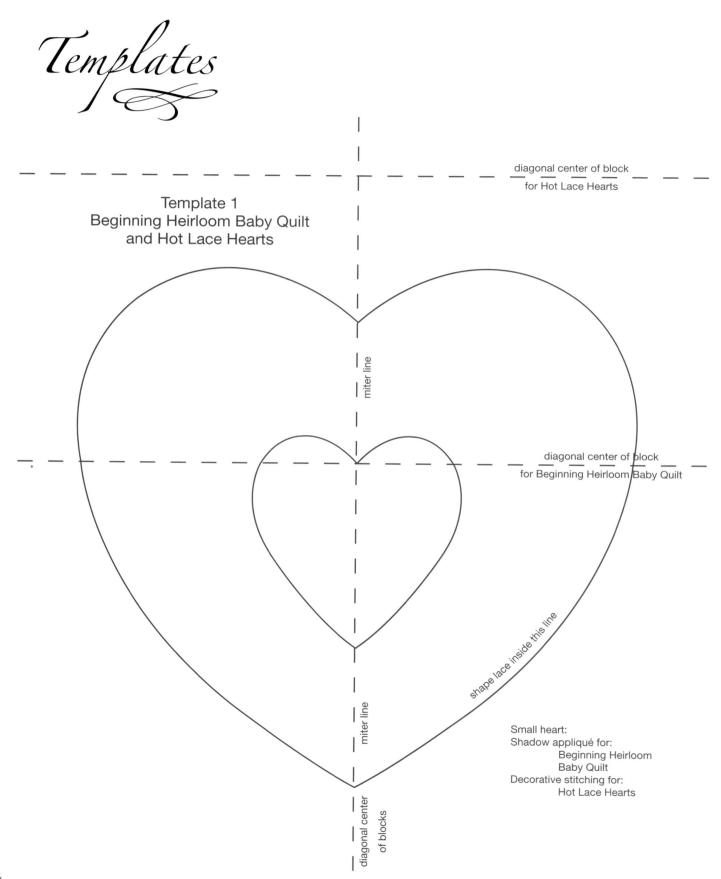

diagonal center of block
for Hot Lace Hearts

Template 1
Beginning Heirloom Baby Quilt
and Hot Lace Hearts

miter line

diagonal center of block
for Beginning Heirloom Baby Quilt

shape lace inside this line

miter line

Small heart:
Shadow appliqué for:
    Beginning Heirloom
    Baby Quilt
Decorative stitching for:
    Hot Lace Hearts

diagonal center
of blocks

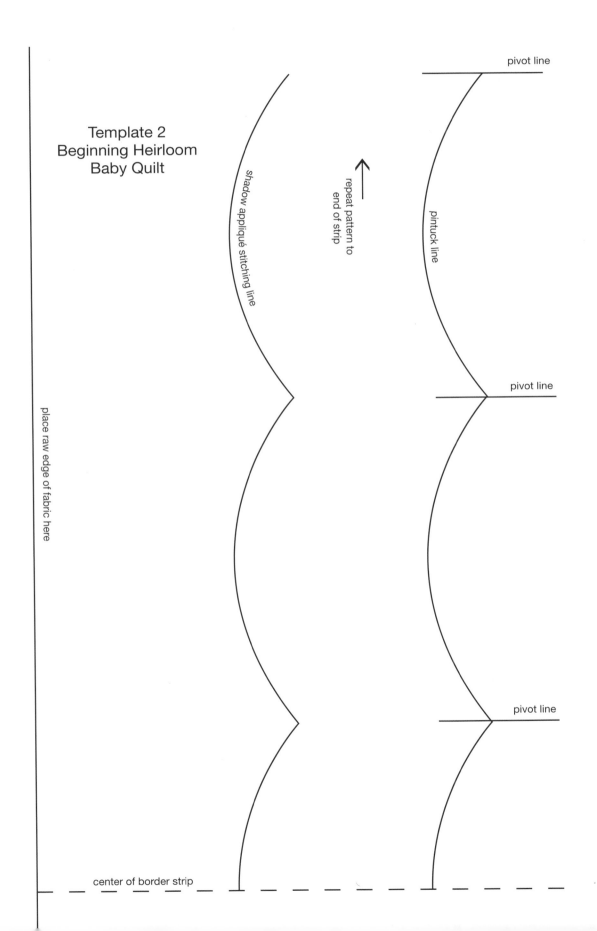

Template 2
Beginning Heirloom
Baby Quilt

shadow appliqué stitching line

repeat pattern to
end of strip

pintuck line

pivot line

pivot line

pivot line

place raw edge of fabric here

center of border strip

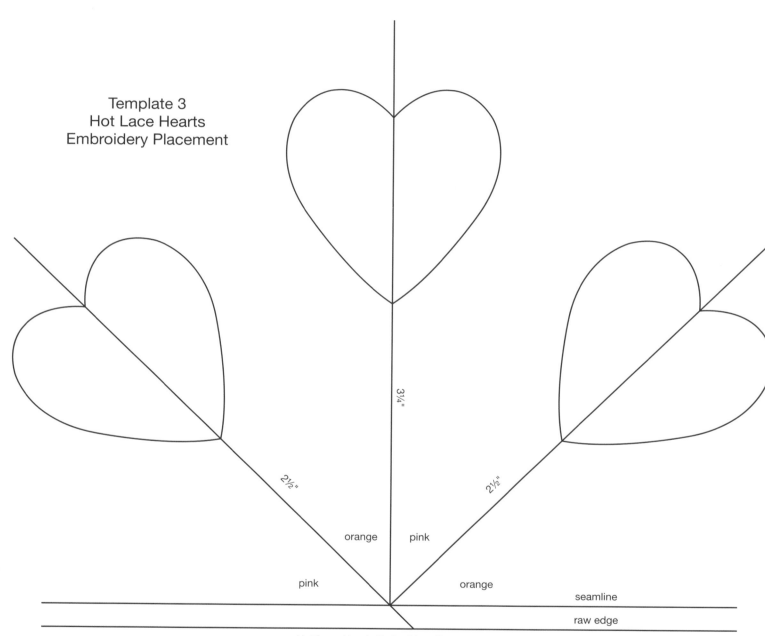

Template 3
Hot Lace Hearts
Embroidery Placement

3¼"

2½"

2½"

orange

pink

pink

orange

seamline

raw edge

Hot Lace Hearts Embroidery Placement

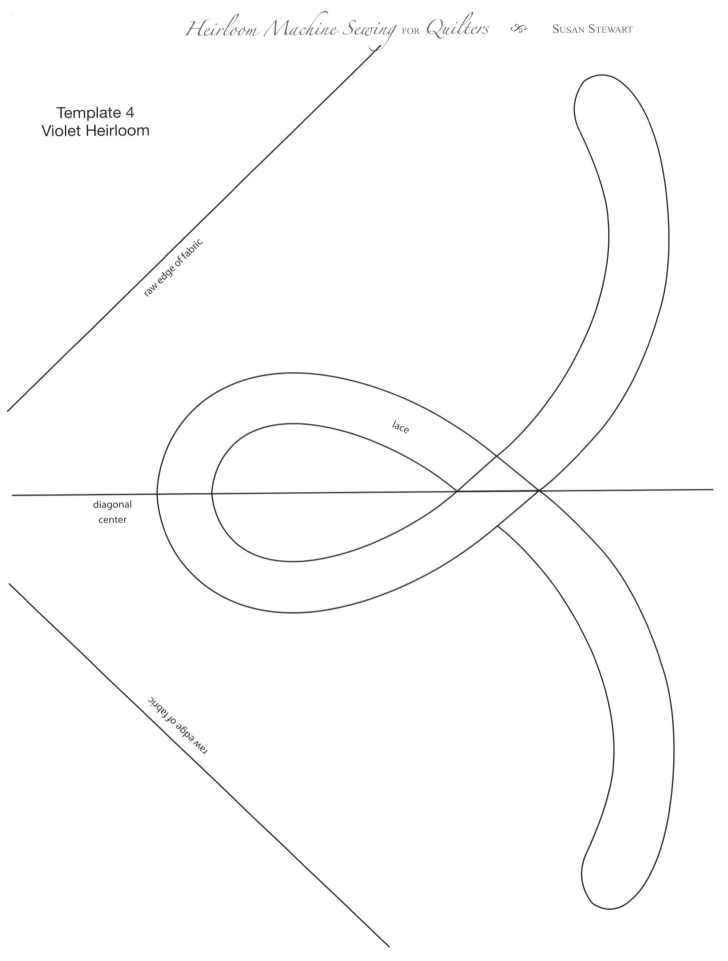

Template 4
Violet Heirloom

raw edge of fabric

lace

diagonal
center

raw edge of fabric

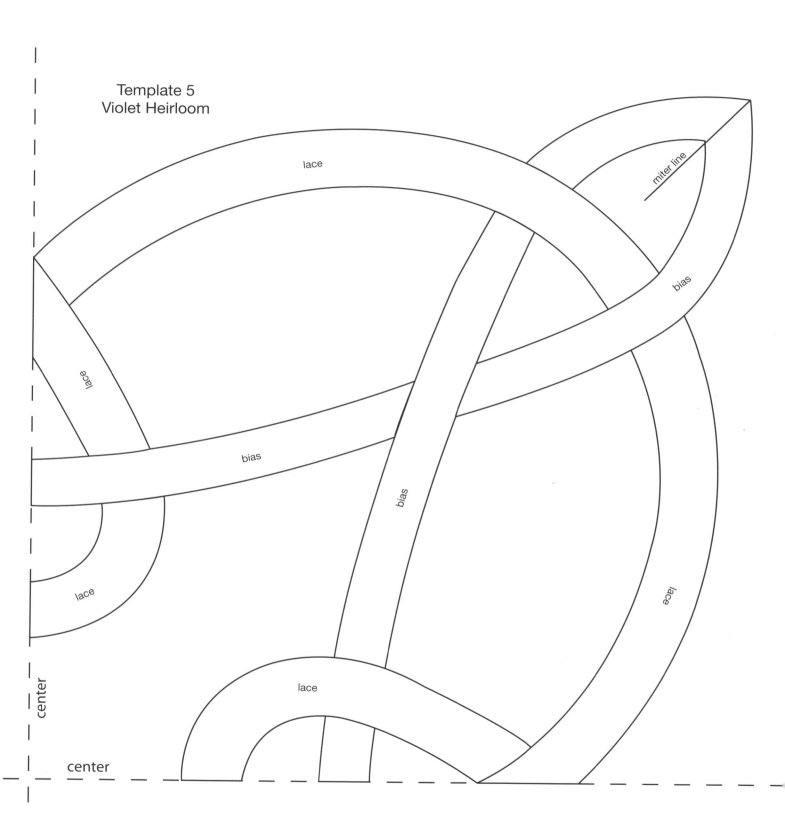

Template 5
Violet Heirloom

lace

miter line

lace

bias

lace

bias

bias

lace

lace

center

center

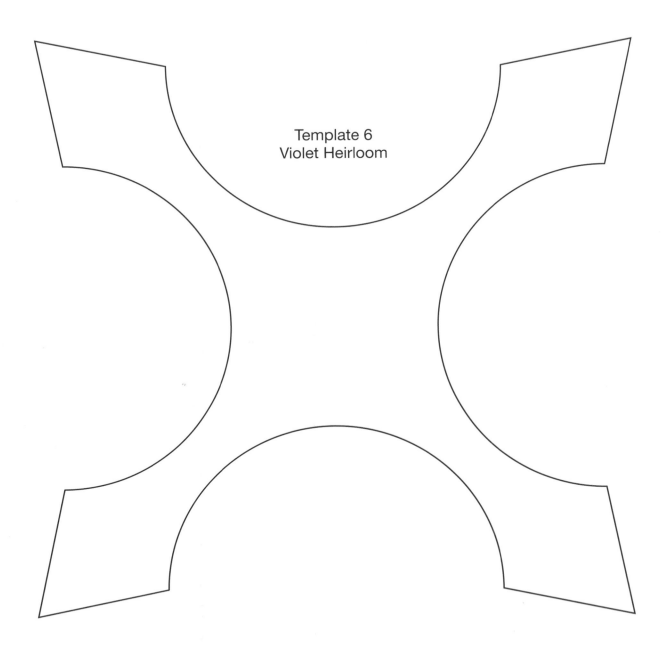

Template 6
Violet Heirloom

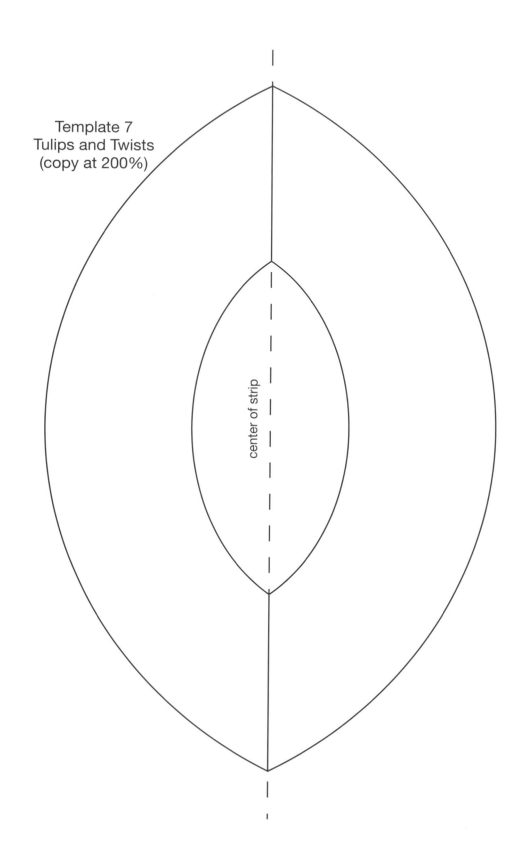

Template 7
Tulips and Twists
(copy at 200%)

center of strip

Template 8
Tulips and Twists

center ─┼─

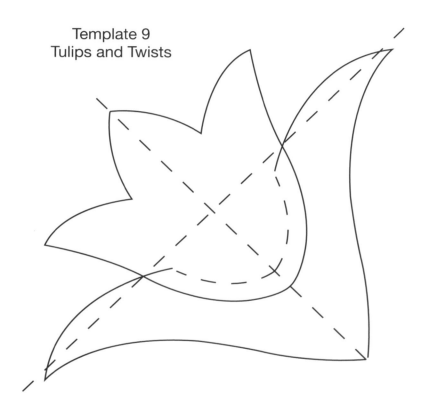

Template 9
Tulips and Twists

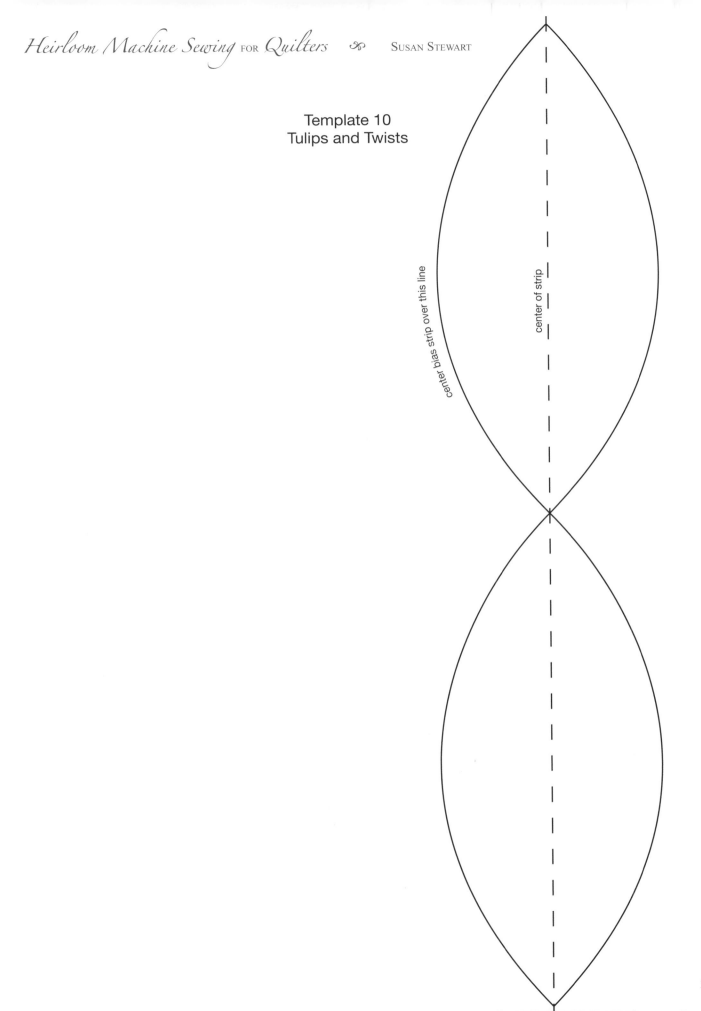

Template 10
Tulips and Twists

center bias strip over this line

center of strip

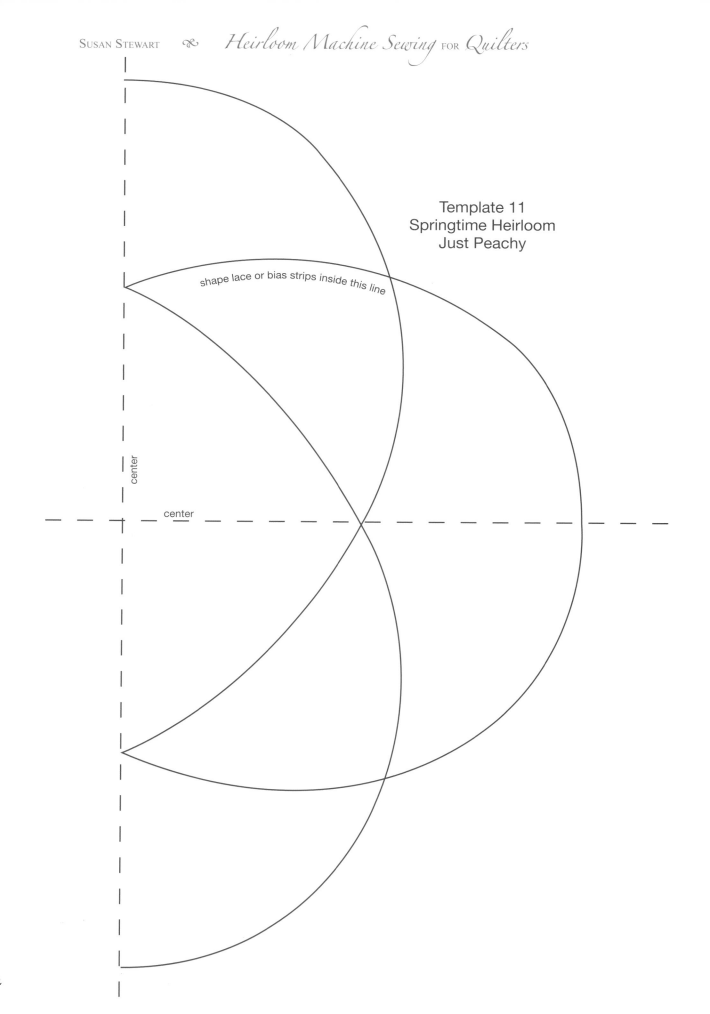

Template 11
Springtime Heirloom
Just Peachy

shape lace or bias strips inside this line

center

center

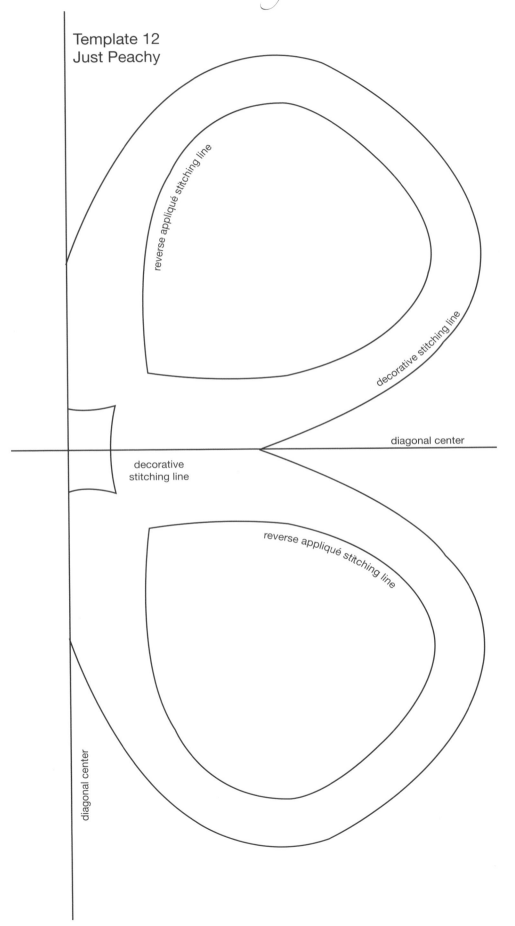

Template 12
Just Peachy

reverse appliqué stitching line

decorative stitching line

diagonal center

decorative
stitching line

reverse appliqué stitching line

diagonal center

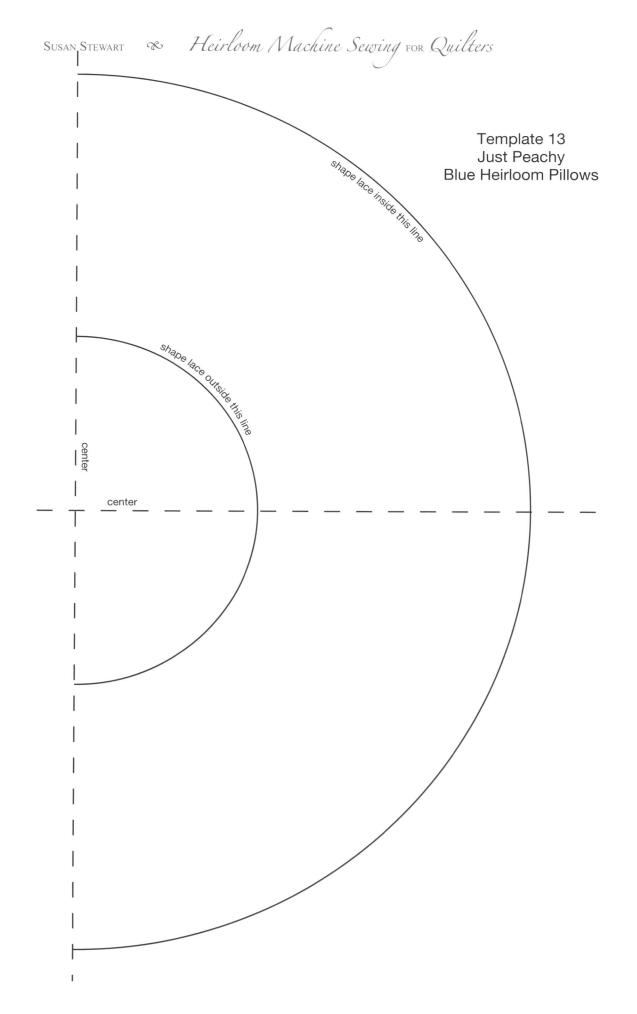

Template 13
Just Peachy
Blue Heirloom Pillows

shape lace inside this line

shape lace outside this line

center

center

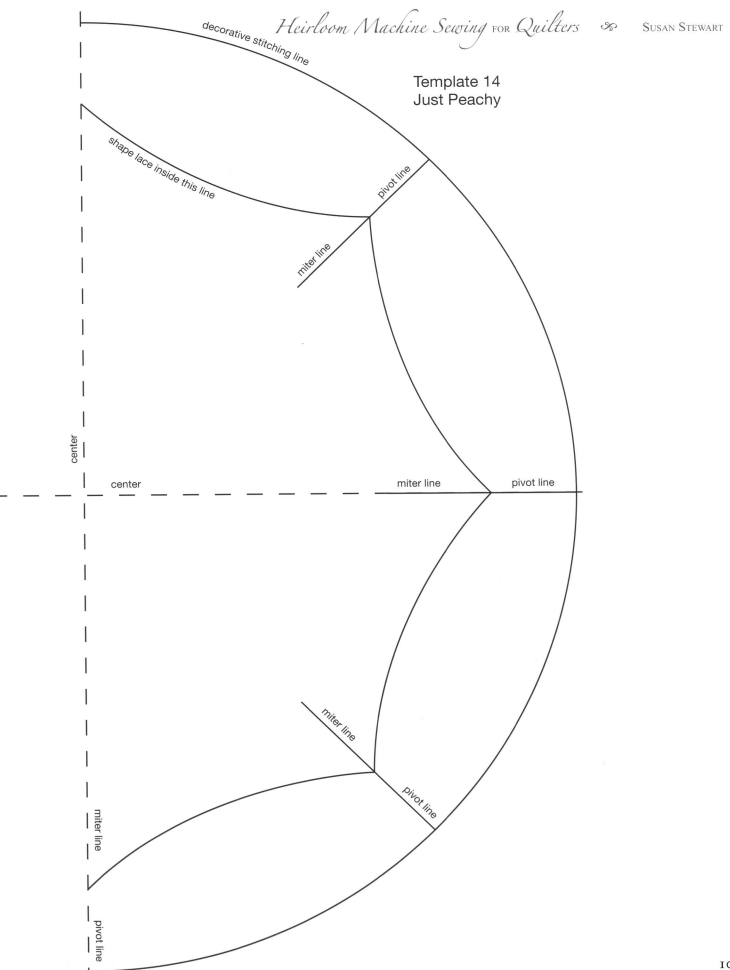

Template 14
Just Peachy

decorative stitching line

shape lace inside this line

pivot line

miter line

center

center

miter line

pivot line

miter line

pivot line

miter line

pivot line

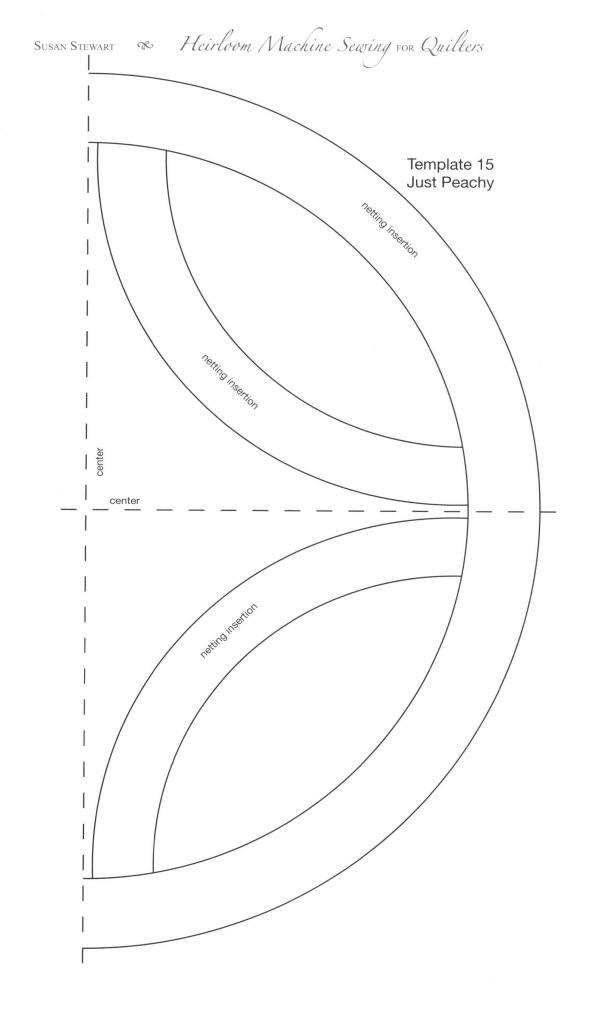

Template 15
Just Peachy

netting insertion

netting insertion

center

center

netting insertion

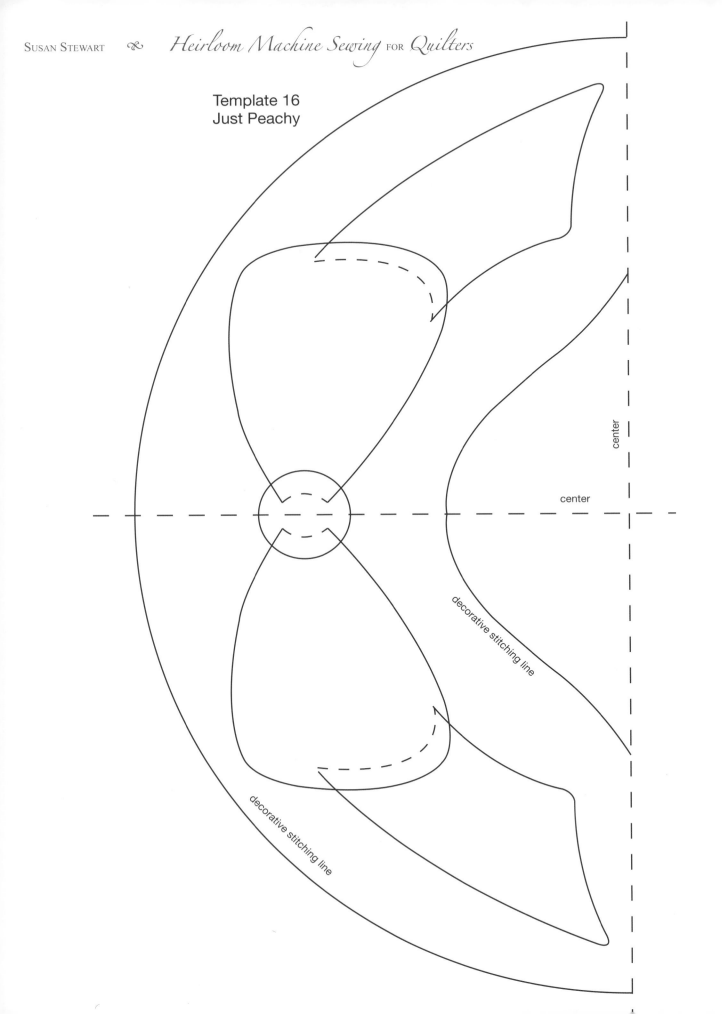

Template 16
Just Peachy

center

center

decorative stitching line

decorative stitching line

Resources

Susan Stewart Designs
Fabric, lace, and project kits
www.SusanStewartDesigns.com
620-232-2936,

Farmhouse Fabrics
Fabric, lace, thread, ribbon, and notions
www.farmhousefabrics.com
803-827-1801 or 888-827-1801

Martha Pullen Company
Fabric, lace, thread, ribbon, and notions
Easy Elegance. Albright & Co., 1996
www.marthapullen.com
800-547-4176,

Wendy Schoen Design
Fabric, lace, and thread
www.wendyschoendesign.com
504-486-9770,

Carol Ahles
Fabric and her revised and expanded book *Fine Machine Sewing*,
2001, Taunton Press
www.carolahles.com
281-558-1496

About the Author

Susan Stewart grew up on a farm in Missouri. She earned a bachelor's degree in chemistry, then worked in immunology research and as a nuclear medicine technologist. After her children were born, she was a stay-at-home mom—and all the while she sewed.

After falling in love with heirloom sewing in 1988, she worked from 1990 to 2005 as a primary designer for the Martha Pullen Company. Sue has had dozens of featured articles in *Sew Beautiful* magazine and wrote *"Sue Says…,"* a tips and tricks column for eight years. Her book *Easy Elegance* featured several of her heirloom design techniques, and she has designed and sold a small line of children's heirloom patterns. She was a regular teacher at the Martha Pullen School of Art Fashion for many years and has also taught for Pfaff and Viking sewing machine dealer conventions and for various sewing groups and guilds.

Recently, her interests have turned toward translating heirloom sewing techniques into quilting. Her heirloom quilts have won awards at American Quilter's Society and International Quilt Association shows. Her quilt HEIRLOOM DREAMS was featured in *Creative Expressions* magazine. Her quilt 94 YARDS OF LACE and the directions for its shark's teeth borders are in Bonnie Browning's book *Borders and Finishing Touches 2* (AQS 2006). As a result of personal experience, Sue has also become interested in providing patterns and supplies for sewing moisture-wicking nightwear for women plagued by night sweats due to menopause or chemotherapy.

Susan lives in Pittsburg, Kansas, with her beloved husband, Mark. She has a grown daughter and son. Honey Dog and Stella Cat keep her company at home while she sews and writes. Check out her Web site at www.SusanStewartDesigns.com

More AQS Books

This is only a small selection of the books available from the American Quilter's Society. AQS books are known worldwide for timely topics, clear writing, beautiful color photos, and accurate illustrations and patterns. The following books are available from your local bookseller, quilt shop, or public library.

#7489   us$24.95

#7496   us$24.95

#7492   us$22.95

#7486   us$22.95

#7074   us$22.95

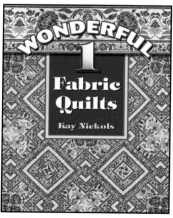

#7487   us$19.95

#7079   us$22.95

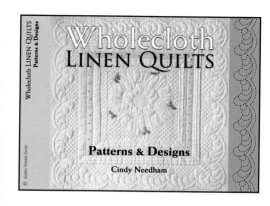

#7485   us$24.95

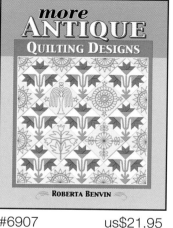

#6907   us$21.95

Look for these books nationally.
Call or **Visit** our Web site at

1-800-626-5420
www.AmericanQuilter.com

110